FREEDOM AND PREJUDICE

FREEDOM AND PREJUDICE

The Legacy of Slavery in the United States and Brazil

Robert Brent Toplin

CONTRIBUTIONS IN AFRO-AMERICAN AND AFRICAN STUDIES, NUMBER 56

GREENWOOD PRESS
Westport, Connecticut • London, England

Library of Congress Cataloging in Publication Data

Toplin, Robert Brent, 1940–
    Freedom and prejudice.

    (Contributions in Afro-American and African studies ;
no. 56 ISSN 0069-9624)
    Bibliography: p.
    Includes index.
    1. Slavery in the United States. 2. Slavery in
Brazil. 3. United States—Race relations. 4. Brazil
—Race relations. I. Title. II. Series.
E441.T67   305.8′00973   80-656
ISBN 0-313-22008-5 (lib. bdg.)

Library of Congress Catalog Card Number: 80-656
ISBN: 0-313-22008-5
ISSN: 0069-9624

First published in 1981

Greenwood Press
A division of Congressional Information Service, Inc.
88 Post Road West, Westport, Connecticut 06881

Printed in the United States of America

10 9 8 7 6 5 4 3 2 1

Contents

Preface

Alexis de Tocqueville, who analyzed American society after nine months travel through the United States, observed that slavery and racial attitudes were intimately connected. Noting that "the abstract and transient fact of slavery is fatally united to the physical and permanent fact of color," he predicted the problem of Negro inequality in America would last long beyond the day of slavery's abolition. Color and servitude were associated in popular attitudes, said Tocqueville, complicating the black man's efforts to take advantage of his emancipation. The tradition of African slavery put a stigma on the Negro, while color distinctions, in turn, perpetuated the tradition of inequality.[1]

What was the source of this prejudice? Did it emerge from a natural distrust in man toward people of different physical appearance? Or was it the product of years of experience in human relationships, whereby Europeans in the New World reserved slavery largely for Africans? The astute Frenchman could give no conclusive answer. His fascinating discussion moved in both directions, citing both the force of color prejudice and the force of bigotry developing out of inequality of condition.

The questions that stirred Tocqueville have interested generations of travelers and scholars. In their search for insights often they have compared race relations in the United States and Brazil. These two societies seemed to offer particularly exciting possibilities for contrast because of the general impression that black-white relationships were more tolerant in Brazil. Perhaps this difference was due to the predominance of class prejudice in Brazil, they conjectured, while color prejudice predominated in the United States. Certainly the two cultures provided a sizeable historical sample for testing the theory through comparison. Brazil and the United States stood out as the giants of the western hemisphere in the history of African slavery and African minorities. By 1860, about four million slaves resided in the United States and almost two million in Brazil. No other nations of the Americas came close to matching these totals. The two societies also experienced the most extensive abolitionist campaigns, tense political crusades that led to abrupt settlements of the slavery problem. Slavery ended in the United States in 1865 after a costly civil war, while it died in Brazil in 1888 following several years of political and social upheaval. In view of these historical parallels it is not surprising that observers have looked especially to the United States and Brazil for clues to understanding the historical background of modern-day race relations. This volume attempts to make a contribution to that search through a study of the tensions that arose out of the quest for emancipation in the nineteenth century and the struggle for racial equality in the twentieth.

The research behind these essays was made possible through the valuable assistance of several institutions. During the last twelve years I have had opportunities to visit libraries and archives across the United States and make four research trips to Brazil. Grants from the National Endowment for the Humanities, the Ford Foundation, the American Philosophical Society, and Denison University facilitated this work immensely. I am also indebted to the many scholars who stirred my thinking about the subject during the initial phases of research. I profited from the insightful questions and commentaries of Samuel Baily, Ira Berlin, Robert Conrad, Emília Viotti da Costa, David Brion Davis, Carl N. Degler, Florestan Fernandes, George M. Fredrickson, Eugene D. Genovese, Sérgio Buarque de Holanda, Octávio Ianni, Thomas E. Skidmore, Stanley J. Stein, and Joel Williamson.

Robert Brent Toplin

Note

1. Alexis de Tocqueville, *Democracy in America*, 2 vols. (New York, 1945) 1:370–96 (quotation, p. 372).

Introduction:
The Legacy of Race
and Class Prejudice

W. E. B. Du Bois summed up the black man's ordeal in America eloquently when he wrote, "One ever feels his twoness—an American, a Negro; two souls, two thoughts, two unreconciled strivings; two warring ideals in one dark body, whose dogged strength alone keeps it from being torn asunder." Much has happened since Du Bois wrote these words in 1903, yet they remain relevant to the subject of race relations. There is still no consensus on the best way for the Afro-American to deal with his "twoness."[1] Some see the tradition of separate identities and cultures as unfortunate. American society needs to desensitize the race issue, they say, and treat all people simply as individual members of the human family. Others see the concept of "twoness" as necessary in a race-conscious society. We cannot hide from the reality of color identification, they argue; rather we should accept our pluralist heritage and encourage our sense of group differences. The movements that emphasize black pride and black consciousness are examples of this trend.

It is not surprising that debates on "twoness" have often led to a discussion of the Brazilian situation. Many observers believed this feeling never disturbed Afro-Brazilians the way it troubled Afro-Americans. They looked excitedly to Brazil as a model of "racial democracy" from which the United States might learn. Robert Allen Christopher summarized the ideal nicely in a 1953 essay, "The Human Race in Brazil." Said Christopher:

Perhaps the most poignant illustration of the difference between the United States and Brazil in the matter of race relations is the fact that a Brazilian Negro generally considers himself first and foremost a *brasileiro* and only second a *preto* (black man). Can the equivalent be said for the U.S. Negro? Far too many, through no fault of their own, cannot help thinking of themselves as Negroes first and U.S. citizens second, which is the real meaning of second class citizenship.[2]

In many respects the contrast Christopher described is still evident in the two societies, despite the progress in America towards civil rights. Racial consciousness remains far stronger in the United States, and scholars have found ample reason to criticize this consciousness as a barrier to progress or praise it as a valuable instrument for combating prejudice. In the process of debating this question about twoness they have delved into history to seek the origins of the differences. Why did the gap between white and black become much wider in the United States, they asked? Which historical conditions created the notable contrasts observed by visitors such as Christopher?

In 1946 historian Frank Tannenbaum excited a lively debate about this question by suggesting that Brazil and the United States had experienced very different kinds of slavery and, as a consequence, dramatic differences developed in postemancipation race relations. The Negro slave in Brazil was recognized fundamentally as a human being, said Tannenbaum, while in the United States he was most fundamentally property. Tannenbaum noted that, "In Latin America the Negro achieved complete legal equality slowly, through manumission, over centuries, and after he had acquired a moral personality. In the United States he was given his freedom suddenly, and before the white community credited him with moral status."[3]

The foundations of Tannenbaum's argument lay in the view that slavery in Latin America was much milder than slavery in the United States. In countries such as Brazil the state and the Roman Catholic Church intervened in master-slave relations to protect the dignity of the slave. Through the force of legal codes and religious tradition, society put a premium on humane treatment. Slaves were not considered merely "things." Latin American law protected the slaves limited rights and facilitated his efforts to purchase freedom. In the United States, however, slavery was more rigid and impersonal.

Slaves were denied opportunities to obtain their freedom; the law did not usually sanctify their marriages or give them access to the courts; and the Protestant churches exhibited much less concern for their souls than did the Roman Catholic Church of Latin America.[4] Differences in the slave systems contributed to differences in racial attitudes after emancipation, argued Tannenbaum. When the challenge of abolition came before Brazilian society, it was not viewed as a catastrophic political crisis. Because the Brazilian Negro already enjoyed some dignity and personal security in slavery, his transition to freedom did not cause alarm. In the United States, where the system created a sizeable gap between slave and citizen, whites were not prepared to begin a new relationship with blacks. The harsh conditions of slavery made black freedom tantamount to revolution, and whites resisted the change violently. In the United States abolition required a long and bloody civil war and was followed by a painful experience with Reconstruction. In Brazil slavery ended in 1888, and there was little racial strife in the aftermath.[5]

The different traditions of slavery affected race relations in the twentieth century, said Tannenbaum. Negroes in the United States faced color barriers at almost every turn, endured legal discrimination, and sometimes suffered the violence of vigilante groups. The racial situation in Brazil was calmer and more fluid. This contrast was most striking in social and sexual relations. White Brazilians openly acknowledged the Negro's contribution to their culture, and many of them judged blacks on the basis of character and ability rather than color. Moreover, miscegenation occurred on a large scale. These differences, "made for a friendly, an elastic milieu within which social change could occur in peace."[6]

During the 1960s and 1970s, many scholars criticized Tannenbaum's assumption about the influence of slavery in shaping modern-day race relations. David Brion Davis and Eugene D. Genovese pointed out commonalities in the slave systems, showing that the masters' harsh or kind treatment or the slaves' rebelliousness or docility depended on a multitude of factors that could develop in any slave society, whether it be Hispanic, Portuguese, British, French, Dutch, or American.[7] Winthrop D. Jordan questioned the effect of slavery on racial attitudes by showing that the Englishmen's hostile impressions of Africans preceded the development of slavery in the British-American colonies.[8] Stanley Stein and Emília Viotti da Costa questioned the myth of mild Brazilian slavery by exposing a sad record of cruel treatment.[9] Florestan Fernandes in turn challenged the view of friendly race relations in the twentieth century by measuring virulent forms of racial bigotry in São Paulo, Brazil.[10] Anthropologist Marvin Harris contributed further to the revision of Tannenbaum by showing the importance of demographic and economic factors in determining race relations.[11]

It remained for Carl N. Degler to integrate these new interpretations and offer the most comprehensive alternative thesis to Tannenbaum's. In *Neither Black Nor White: Slavery and Race Relations in Brazil and the United states* (1971) Degler brilliantly summarized the new scholarship and added his own insights from an informed reading of the primary materials. By means of a broad overview of the two countries' histories, Degler questioned Tannenbaum's view of the connections between slavery and racism.

Degler began his assault on the Tannenbaum thesis by carefully distinguishing between the theory and the practice of slavery. He showed that legal codes supposedly designed to protect the slaves in Brazil had little effect in day-to-day life. Rules promulgated by the church and state did not carry much weight on the plantations, where proprietors governed relatively free from outside interference. Indeed, the humanitarian practices Tannenbaum described, such as protecting slave marriages and guaranteeing the slave's right to save money to purchase his freedom, were given strong legal sanction only in the last years of slavery in Brazil, when the pressures of abolitionism forced reform. Before the 1870s and 1880s, the life of many Brazilian slaves was brutish and short. Slave mortality rates were high because of disease, poor living standards, and the hard work demanded of Negroes in the Brazilian fields and mines.

When Degler turned to North American slavery, he exploded other myths. Degler maintained that the system in the United States did not compare as invidiously to Latin America as Tannenbaum suggested. In fact, the formal definition of the slave's status in the United States and Brazil was quite similar. In both societies the law treated slaves paradoxically. Slaves were both human beings and property. There were differences in physical treatment, however, particularly because of the Atlantic slave trade. The United States closed its doors officially to the vicious traffic in 1808, while Brazil procrastinated until 1850. Contact with the trade meant continued importation of cheap African laborers who were badly exploited for a short period and then replaced with new captives. The trade also affected the male-female sex ratio in the slave community. Brazil's long-term association with the trade brought a disproportionately large number of males into the slave population. In the United States, on the other hand, there was greater dependence on natural reproduction to augment the slave population, a situation that facilitated the growth of slave marriages and families. Differences showed up in the list of daily provisions too. Degler discovered that the food and shelter provided for North American slaves was generally superior to the provisions for Latin American bondsmen.[12]

It was in the category of race relations, not slavery, that Degler found a harsher situation in the United States. The contrast was especially evident in the way slaveholders viewed free Negroes and mulattoes. Whites in the American South feared the colored freedmen. They were worried that the freed slaves were a potential danger to the security of slavery. They believed that color sentiment could make them allies of the slaves in the event of escapes or rebellions. Southern slaveholders were apprehensive, also, about race relations after abolition. They feared that emancipation for millions of black slaves would quickly degenerate into a bloody racial struggle.

In Brazil leaders displayed little apprehension about the free Negroes. In fact, by the nineteenth century, there were more free coloreds than slaves in Brazil, and white proprietors counted on these people to give security to the slave system. Many of the free coloreds served as slavecatchers for the planters or as marginal field workers during the planting and harvest seasons. White proprietors especially trusted the mulattoes as their allies and gave them preferred treatment. Mulattoes showed little emotional interest in their black brothers in bondage. Thus, the Brazilian situation lacked the explosive sense of racial identification that stirred fear in the United States and inspired some white leaders to call for the colonization of free blacks in Africa or Central America. The Brazilians more readily accepted freedmen as new members of the free citizenry. What are the origins of these differences? Again, Degler emphasizes that they emerged from different historical experiences, not different systems of slavery. Colonial Brazil had difficulty attracting Portuguese immigrants, and many of those who did come were single males. As Brazil's slave population grew to substantial size, sexual relations between Portuguese men and slave women became extensive. The offspring of these relationships and their later descendants established themselves in the economy, including positions that bolstered the slave regime. On the other hand British America had a tradition of reserving marginal economic places for whites. The trend developed early. Degler reminds us that racial sentiments in England predated the growth of British slavery in America, and he notes that this problem of prejudice was compounded by the colonial pattern of settlement. White immigrants, including many white families, represented the bulk of settlers in the early growth of the colonial South. This situation made miscegenation less frequent than in Brazil's first years, and it gave poor whites virtual monopolies over the marginal occupations, including the job of slavecatcher. These poor whites viewed the free blacks as potential competitors for their small privileges. The dichotomy between opportunities for whites and free blacks encouraged the hardening of attitudes toward color. Whites, whether rich or poor, came to see themselves as members of the master class. Many poor whites believed they had a strong stake in the system of slavery even though they were not themselves slaveholders.

Degler sees the North Americans' fear of *both* the black slave and the black freedman as an important clue in understanding the very different ways the two societies responded to the challenge of abolition. Whites in the American South defended slavery in racial terms, speaking of biological differences between color groups and worrying that "white civilization" could be destroyed by hordes of free blacks. But white Brazilians could not muster a racial defense of slavery; the Brazilian context made a rigid racial ideology unworkable. Brazilian society already included great numbers of free Negroes and mixed-bloods, including prominent mulattoes who owned slaves and held important political positions. Brazilian slaveholders could defend their institution as a necessary evil, but they could hardly attempt the strict racial argument that excited North Americans.

As Brazilian society moved into the postemancipation era, the tradition of special treatment for mulattoes gave visitors to Brazil the impression that the country's racial system was calm and friendly. Brazil's multicategory approach to identifying color groups made the danger of racial confrontations far less likely than in the United States. In Brazilian society mulattoes were especially subject to co-option by whites. They had access to a "mulatto escape-hatch," said Degler. Lighter-skinned mulattoes enjoyed greater social acceptance and economic opportunity than the darker-skinned individuals. Mulattoes who acquired wealth, education, and good clothes might climb close to the highest echelons of society. Once these mulattoes "arrived," they did not care to look back. The presence of some Brazilian lightskins in the upper strata served nicely for advertising Brazil to outsiders as a "racial democracy." No racial problem here, said the Brazilian elites as they compared themselves favorably to North Americans. In the meantime the mass of dark-skinned Brazilians remained trapped at the bottom of the Brazilian economy and society, and they lacked the racial solidarity necessary to challenge the situation.[13]

In the United States, abolition represented a much more serious threat to the social system. A strong heritage of democratic rule had developed from its foundations in the colonial period, and in the Jacksonian era the principal of universal white manhood suffrage won wide approval. This democratic tradition gave Southern whites nightmares after the Civil War as they contemplated the enfranchisement of a huge black electorate. They had good reason to worry. Blacks naturally joined ranks with their Republican friends during Reconstruction, and, for a short time, a coalition of blacks and white Republicans controlled the political machinery. Furthermore, there was no "mulatto escape hatch" to divide the South's black population. All Southern blacks were potentially brothers in the biracial system that identified even the very light mulatto as "Negro" and subject to second-class citizenship.

North America's different historical experience with race relations produced a far more rigid color division than in Brazilian society. After the brief period of moderate progress for blacks during Reconstruction, Southern whites secured control again. By the early twentieth century whites had succeeded in establishing a new form of quasi-slavery. Legal and extralegal intimidation separated the blacks and made them subordinate. Jim Crow laws, court rulings, political disenfranchisement, sharecropping, KKK violence, lynch mobs, and a variety of other tactics accomplished the task. Racial ideology, including variations of the old proslavery thought, helped to justify the pattern of inequality.

In racial terms, then, the situation in the United States led to a severe division between black and white, while in Brazil the mulatto escape hatch developed as a part of a less rigid racial division. Color and class prejudice existed in Brazil, but the society's more flexible sense of racial differences, which had matured over several centuries, left little need for a rigid ideology. Thus, concluded Degler, variations in historical experience, not a different kind of slavery, explained the contrasts in present-day Brazil and the United States.[14]

Two years after the appearance of Degler's study sociologist Harmannus Hoetink published an important work that attempted to carry revisions of the Tannenbaum thesis a step further. Hoetink questioned not only Tannenbaum's assumption that different slave systems had produced different race relations; he also challenged the view that differences in modern-day race relations were primarily the result of distinct economic and cultural factors.[15] Hoetink left no major researcher unscathed. In a variety of ways he criticized the theories of Carl N. Degler, Marvin Harris, Florestan Fernandes, Winthrop D. Jordan, and others and then tried to erect his own broad scheme of analysis over the wreckage. Hoetink's most provocative contribution to the debates was his research on the connection between sexual relations and attitudes toward race relations. Hoetink treated views toward miscegenation and interracial marriage as particularly revealing indicators of the status of race relations. He argued that there were, indeed, major differences between multiracial societies in the Americas. Tannenbaum was right about the greater liberality of Iberian society towards race, but the key to the difference was not slavery.

In *Slavery and Race Relations in the Americas: Comparative Notes on Their Nature and Nexus* Hoetink noted the commonality of racial prejudice in the Americas. It was evident in every multiracial society of the western hemisphere. Bigotry took different forms in different cultures, but it was nevertheless significant and pervasive. Why was this common denominator of prejudice present? The problem related to the "somatic norm image," said Hoetink. This image was the ideal of physical beauty that prevailed in each society. The dominant social group, the whites, typically defined this archetype in terms of their own physical qualities, while the darkskinned groups internalized the European model of attractiveness. In Hispanic, Portuguese, Dutch, French, and British cultures many Negroes displayed a preference for lighter color and European physical features. The attitude was particularly noticeable in the way darkskinned individuals preferred lighter-skinned partners for dating, sexual relations, and marriage.

While Brazil and Hispanic America shared this racial orientation with other societies of the Americas, there was an important difference, noted Hoetink. The Iberian whites showed "greater willingness to enter into sexual relations on the basis of social acceptance with persons from the lighter colored middle groups." For example, many white Brazilian males engaged unashamedly in romantic relationships with light-colored women and recognized the children from their relationships with pride and responsibility. If the women possessed unusual beauty or good social, economic, and educational background, it was not unusual for the man to consider marriage. In Brazil, as in Spanish America, the somatic norm image permitted some flexibility in accepting light-colored individuals into the top group.[16]

This narrowing of the somatic distance between whites and light coloreds was much less evident in the British, Dutch, and French societies of the Americas. It is true, of course, that in the Caribbean area males of Northwest European background engaged frequently in sexual liaisons with mulatto women and gave mulattoes preferred treatment, but they did not usually consider mulattoes appropriate marriage mates even when the individuals were of great physical beauty or high class status. In short the British, French, and Dutch Caribbean developed a three-tiered racial system that awarded mulattoes a higher social level than Negroes but failed to give mulattoes easy mobility into the top racial classification.

In the continental United States the racial division appeared in two parts rather than three. The two-tier system defined individuals simply as black or white and provided no significant intermediate status for mulattoes. Light coloreds were lumped together with their Negro brethren, and the tremendous "social distance" between them and the whites discouraged thoughts of acceptance into the dominant group. No combination of physical attractiveness or financial standing could win a light mulatto identification with the white reference group.[17]

Although Hoetink succeeded in throwing new light on the contrasts between Iberian and Northwest European societies, he did not provide a detailed historical explanation for the roots of the difference. His perceptive cross-cultural analysis of current conditions was not supported with groundbreaking historical evidence on the sources of the contrast. Hoetink left his readers to ask: *Why* did the Iberian societies develop a more liberal view of relations between whites and mulattoes? Why did many British, Dutch, and French societies of the Caribbean develop a three-tier color system, while the United States developed a two-tier system? Hoetink's explanations did not carry the scholarship much beyond the earlier work of Degler, Harris, Jordan, Fernandes, and other scholars who made important contributions to the debates.

Somewhere in the *history* of multiracial societies of the Americas lay the sources of the differences. As many students of race relations have already observed, variations in racial attitudes may have emerged from differences already present in Europe before colonization of the Americas. Varying patterns of colonial settlement also affected attitudes and behavior. The ratio of white Europeans to African slaves and the ratio of single males to families influenced patterns of miscegenation, and the development of large-scale plantation societies also affected conditions. Political traditions helped shape race relations, too. The poor whites in democratic societies typically feared competition from emancipated slaves more than poor whites in hierarchical societies. Finally, and particularly important in terms of the interpretations explored in this volume, patterns in modern-day race relations have been shaped, to a degree, by the history of slavery and its abolition.

American and Brazilian scholars readily acknowledge that the tumultuous period of abolition made a profound impact on the economy and politics of the two societies. Can the same be said for race relations? The general question prompts some specific ones. Was racial prejudice more or less evident during the political crises over abolition? Did slaveholders fear slave violence because of tensions over abolition or tensions over race? Why did blacks in both societies face great obstacles in turning their new freedom into an instrument for mobility? Was racial bigotry their greatest barrier to progress, or another legacy of slavery—their class position?

Degler and Hoetink stress the importance of racial factors. Their investigations suggest that attitudes toward color were the major force in determining differences in status and power between racial groups. Degler finishes, for example, with a discussion captioned, "Always That Indelible Color." He observes that "Physical differences between groups are always noticed," and states his conviction "that blacks will be recognized as different and discriminated against whenever nonblacks will have the power and incentive to do so. So long as men perceive identifying physical differences that can be used to discriminate against another group, they will do so."[18] What, then, can be done to combat racial inequality? As race prejudice emerged from awareness of physical differences, economic and educational improvement for the Negro cannot naturally destroy the irrational basis for antipathy, just as laws against segregation and discrimination cannot alone accomplish the task. The pervasive problem of color prejudice must be met head-on by teaching people *not* to be prejudiced, says Degler.[19] Similarly, Hoetink stresses the centrality of attitudes toward color. He observes that all multiracial societies in the Americas are influenced by the "racist selection principal" and notes that once patterns in race relations take shape, they show remarkable resiliency and resistance to change.[20] Hoetink's recommendations for fighting color prejudice are less specific than Degler's. He calls for further understanding of the phenomenon of prejudice through comparative research, hoping that each society can "become better aware of the direction into which it is moving and of the chances, if any, of changing its course."[21]

Unquestionably, Degler and Hoetink have helped greatly to show how color sensitivity affects relationships, but their tendency to downplay the influence of slavery and, ultimately, class in molding racial attitudes leads to difficulties. The pendulum of revisionist research has swung so far over that the significant interplay between race and class factors has been underestimated. No doubt, color prejudice is a potent force in its own right, but it is often greatly affected by the environment in which it grows. The historical record shows that attitudes towards color were never fixed in either society; they evolved and were shaped by the forces of change.

Part I of this volume focuses on the period of transition from slavery to freedom and discusses the way tensions over abolition pushed loosely articulated racial concepts into the open and gave them the force of formal ideology. As pressures toward abolition grew in the United States and Brazil, defenders of the status quo eagerly reached for racial concepts to defend their endangered institution. Ideas about the inferiority of Negroes gained in prominence and acceptability. Even attitudes toward mulattoes were affected by the political turmoil. In the American South resistance to abolitionists led to a reconsideration of the traditional preference for mulattoes. Hence, racial attitudes were in flux in the United States and Brazil during the crises over slavery, and the new trends appear to have made a major impact on relations between blacks and whites in the period after emancipation.

Part II deals with the process of abolition and raises related questions about the force of color prejudice in creating tensions. In recent decades research in the United States has put emphasis on the significance of racial antipathy in the secession crisis. This revisionist history has been greatly influenced by the twentieth-century civil rights struggle and the racial violence that attended it. Allan Nevins signaled the trend in his *Ordeal of the Union* (1947). Nevins traced Southern white intransigence to a fear of "race adjustment" after emancipation.[22] More recently, Steven Channing (1970) stressed that "race fear" was a fundamental concern of leading South Carolina secessionists.[23]

Although the anticipation of racial conflict excited secessionist sentiment in the South, we should recall that the *condition* of blacks also caused tensions. Blacks were feared not just because of their race but also because they were an enslaved people who someday, under the right conditions, might rebel against the system. Where slavery became deeply rooted, as in the plantation societies of the United States and Brazil, it involved coercion over great numbers of laborers, and there could be no major alterations in the master's authority without seriously jeopardizing the machinery of control. In the eyes of the slaveholders, government interference in the form of emancipation laws could lead to great trouble. In this respect resistance to abolition in the United States and Brazil was similar. Like their North American counterparts, Brazilian slaveholders fought abolition with nervous predictions of violence and anarchy. Brazilians did not show the same fear of race war, but they did shout the familiar warning that abolition could bring the downfall of the economic, social, and political order to which they were deeply committed. They sounded very much like the slaveholders of Dixie in their claims that abolitionism was an "incendiary" movement that might reach the slave quarters and bring great civil disorder.

Although the *institution* of slavery finally passed from the two societies, the *traditions* remained. The legacy of slavery, which concerned both race and class attitudes, complicated the efforts of Afro-Americans and Afro-Brazilians to improve themselves. A heritage of color prejudice was passed down, and so, too, was a tradition of economic inequality. Lack of property, inadequate job skills, and shortcomings in education represented major impediments for the freedmen and their descendants. In both the United States and Brazil generations of blacks were trapped in the culture of poverty and without easy access to economic opportunity.

Part III shows that many observers were greatly impressed with superficial differences between American and Brazilian society in the twentieth century and that consequently they failed to appreciate the important interrelationship between race and class prejudice. They assumed that racial attitudes were fundamental in establishing black inequality in the United States, while class attitudes predominated in Brazil. But recent scholarship has brought the factors into greater balance and helped to reveal important common denominators. Students of Brazilian race relations such as Thomas E. Skidmore, Thales de Azevedo, and Florestan Fernandes exposed the myth of "racial democracy" and measured the force of color prejudice in Brazilian society.[24] They found much informal racial discrimination and showed that many Brazilians used the "whitening ideal" to downplay their culture's African heritage. Frequently, white Brazilians stressed the importance of miscegenation in lightening the national complexion, thus engaging in a subtle form of prejudice that was better tailored to Brazilian history and demography than the pattern of descent-rule that appeared in the United States.

On the other side of the coin, some recent research has placed renewed emphasis on the importance of class prejudice in creating obstacles to progress for blacks in the United States. The evidence reminds us that problems related to condition can be as troublesome as problems related to color.[25]

Economist Thomas Sowell offers intriguing comments along these lines by placing the black experience against the background of other cultures and other periods of history. In *Race and Economics* (1975) Sowell considers the condition of many present-day blacks analogous to the situation of immigrants who arrived in America between 1840 and 1924.[26] He finds the parallels with the Irish particularly relevant. Most Irishmen came to America in the nineteenth century from rural backgrounds. They were illiterate, unskilled, and inexperienced in the customs that could facilitate adaptation to life in the large metropolitan areas. Consequently, their early adjustment to the urban environment proved difficult and painful.

Sowell believes that conditions for many blacks in twentieth-century America were not very different from conditions for the Irish in the nineteenth. The black migration to large cities began during World War I and accelerated significantly during and after World War II. Historically speaking, this massive migration was a relatively recent phenomenon. Because so many blacks came out of poor and isolated rural communities in the South, the problems that they and their children faced in the tense and impersonal city environment hardly seem surprising. In the long run, the record of the Irish suggests that prospects for blacks are more sanguine than the pessimists believe. Whereas many Americans considered the Irish hopeless slum-dwellers not many generations ago, today the Irish are generally regarded as a well-assimilated minority group. The term "Irishman" once conveyed negative connotations in street language and barroom talk, but today it invokes positive images. In popular thought today's Irishman is a bona fide mainstream American with a proud ethnic heritage. Will the same hold true for blacks? Perhaps this pattern is already recurring. While more and more blacks move into middle-income jobs, other "newcomers" or immigrants such as

Mexican-Americans move to the cities and take the places blacks monopolized earlier. The familiar historical process grinds on.

Many would debate whether today's upwardly mobile blacks can find the same welcome that eventually applied to successful Irishmen. They consider the blacks' problem of "twoness" more severe than anything the Irish ever faced. Color and race block the black man's path, not just class position, they argue. Racial prejudice has shown a strange resiliency over the course of history that economic and educational improvement cannot easily overcome.

This fundamental debate about the impact of race and class prejudice is not likely to conclude in the foreseeable future. As long as scholars continue to find evidence indicating that both problems are at work in fostering inequality, there will be excited claims about the predominance of one or the other. If the research in this volume reveals anything, it is that both factors need to be addressed if the American and Brazilian societies are to confront the wrongs perpetrated against people of African descent. The irrational and ethnocentric phenomenon of color prejudice requires continued attention, and so, too, does the problem of class inequality that emerged with the experience of slavery.

Notes

1. W. E. B. Du Bois, *The Souls of Black Folk*, in *Three Negro Classics* (New York, 1965), p. 215.

2. Robert Allen Christopher, "The Human Race in Brazil," *Americas* (July 1953), pp. 3–31.

3. Frank Tannenbaum, *Slave and Citizen: The Negro in the Americas* (New York, 1946), p. 112.

4. Ibid., pp. 39–90.

5. Ibid., pp. 91–113.

6. Ibid., pp. viii, 113–28.

7. Eugene D. Genovese, "Rebelliousness and Docility in the Negro Slave: A Critique of the Elkins Thesis," in Ann J. Lane, ed., *The Debate Over Slavery: Stanley Elkins and His Critics* (Urbana, 1971), pp. 43–75; David Brion Davis, *The Problem of Slavery in Western Culture* (Ithaca, 1966).

8. Winthrop D. Jordan, *White Over Black: American Attitudes Toward the Negro, 1550-1812* (Chapel Hill, N.C., 1968).

9. Stanley Stein, *Vassouras: A Brazilian Slave County, 1850-1900* (Cambridge, Mass., 1957); Emília Viotti da Costa, *Da senzala à côlonia* (São Paulo, 1966).

10. Florestan Fernandes, *A integração do negro a sociedade de classes,* 2 vols. (São Paulo, 1964).

11. Marvin Harris, *Patterns of Race Relations in the Americas* (New York, 1964).

12. Carl N. Degler, *Neither Black Nor White: Slavery and Race Relations in Brazil and the United States* (New York, 1971), pp. 25-82.

13. Ibid., pp. 16-21, 43-47, 75-92, 213-56.

14. Ibid., pp. 256-64.

15. H. Hoetink, *Slavery and Race Relations in the Americas: Comparative Studies on Their Nature and Nexus* (New York, 1973). His earlier work is also an important contribution: *Caribbean Race Relations: A Study of Two Variants* (New York, 1971).

16. Hoetink, *Slavery and Race Relations in the Americas,* pp. 192-210.

17. Ibid., pp. 3-28.

18. Degler, *Neither Black Nor White,* p. 287.

19. Ibid., pp. 287-92.

20. Hoetink, *Slavery and Race Relations in the Americas,* pp. 25-28.

21. Ibid., p. 210.

22. Allan Nevins, *The Ordeal of the Union,* 8 vols. (New York, 1947), 1: 509-30.

23. Steven Channing, *Crisis of Fear: Secession in South Carolina* (New York, 1970).

24. Thomas E. Skidmore, *Black into White: Race and Nationality in Brazilian Thought* (New York, 1974); Thales de Azevedo, *Democracia racial: ideologia e realidade* (Petropolis, 1975); Florestan Fernandes, *The Negro in Brazilian Society* (New York, 1971).

25. For a relevant general analysis of the interrelationships between race prejudice and class prejudice, see Pierre van den Berghe, *Race and Racism: A Comparative Perspective* (New York, 1967).

26. Thomas Sowell, *Race and Economics* (New York, 1975).

PART 1:
TRANSFORMATIONS
IN RACIAL ATTITUDES

Proslavery, Anti-Black: The Hardening of Racial Attitudes in the Antebellum South

Thus, Dear Sir, when arguments fail, an
entrenchment is made behind prejudice alone.[1]
—John Jones to James Gillespie Birney,
July 25, 1835

Racial thought was not fixed in the early years of the American republic; it changed considerably, and these transformations gave evidence of an important connection between slavery and racism. During the period of the Revolution and the Constitution, national leaders rarely or only vaguely voiced a racial defense of slavery. The spirit of the Enlightenment was in fashion as expressed in Thomas Jefferson's claim in the Declaration of Independence that "all men are created equal." In this context an environmentalist view of the black man prevailed. Slavery, not race, was the primary factor in forming the Negro's character, said the observers. They spoke of slavery's debilitating effects, claiming that free blacks were less educated than whites and more troubled by poverty because of their experience in bondage and because of the social stigma placed on them by the public's association of color with servitude. This cultural explanation for social differences eventually gave way to a racial explanation, however. More and more, defenders of slavery insisted that blacks were fundamentally inferior to whites in physical, mental, and moral endowment. In this manner proslavery and anti-Negro thought developed along roughly parallel courses, a pattern that reflected the function of racism in the defense of slavery.[2] Environmentalist viewpoints clearly dominated speculation about Negro character during the period of the Revolution and the Enlightenment. In most public discussions during the 1770-1810 period the principle of the inherent equality of all men was assumed to be fundamentally valid. Frequently, discussants invoked the authority of the Declaration of Independence to make this point, affirming that "all men are created equal." They treated Jefferson's memorable phrase as an almost unassailable statement of national ideals. Commentators acknowledged that the personality and character of slaves and free blacks reflected degrading living conditions, but this observation did not undermine their faith in the fundamental oneness of origins. Whether they viewed the subject through the lens of religion, with emphasis on the Creation, or of the Enlightenment, with emphasis on Nature, they continued to pay formal respect to the ideal of equality.[3]

Environmentalism nicely served the purposes of the individuals who tried to stir moral conscience in the interest of emancipation. Anthony Benezet, a Quaker and one of the foremost early American critics of slavery, stressed the reform implications of words in the Declaration of Independence. If all men were created equal, he reasoned, the inherent injustices of slavery needed correction. There was only one way to deny this conclusion, thought Benezet: to prove that Africans were not men.[4] The Reverend Samuel Stanhope Smith pressed this argument more specifically by attributing almost all major Negro characteristics to nurture, not nature. In his book, *An Essay on the Causes and the Variety of Complexion and Figure in the Human Species*, Smith traced the origins of blacks and whites to a common biblical source, Adam and Eve. Arguing that all mankind developed from a uniform human species, he related the physical differences between blacks and whites to the varying natural environments in which they lived. Climatic factors were especially important to Smith. The sun caused dark pigmentation, he explained, and the Negro's supposedly greater tendency to perspire had developed as a cooling function to allow long work in hot weather.[5]

The racial views of prominent Southern slaveholders in the period did not clash dramatically with the concepts of Benezet,

Smith, and other environmentalists. Slave proprietors who spoke publicly about slavery, including members of Virginia's planter elite, frequently apologized for the peculiar institution and lamented its unfortunate effects on both blacks and whites. Slavery shackled the blacks, created tense and unnatural relationships between the races, and encouraged laziness among the whites, they said. Hopefully, someday, another generation might find opportunities to extricate itself from the problem. But for the present, there seemed little choice but to accept life's realities and live with the unpleasant system. Slavery was, in the familiar phrase, an "evil necessity."[6] Environmentalists from the Northern states welcomed these Southern comments on the shortcomings of slavery. The Southerners' statements gave impressive testimony, emanating directly from the whites who were closest to the black bondsmen, to support their view that slavery was the prime cause of prejudice.

If abolitionism had developed into a significant threat to Southern slavery in the late eighteenth century, the relaxed and apologetic reflections on slavery might have transformed swiftly into a hardened, more abstractly defensive, and even racial case against emancipation. But a serious threat never emerged. As Robert McColley, David Brion Davis, and other historians have shown, the chest-pounding acknowledgments of the evil of slavery were not accompanied by strong legislative efforts to free the South's bondsmen. Many talked about reform, but few acted on it. On the individual level, some proprietors manumitted their slaves, yet these personal decisions, whether motivated by philanthropy or economics, did not substantially reduce the overall slave population or inspire a major political assault on the institution. Slavery was not dying in Jeffersonian Virginia. "The antislavery arguments of the Revolution period were notably abstract and seldom touched on the actual condition, interests or future of Negro Americans," concludes David Brion Davis.[7]

During the early national period, on a few occasions, individuals attempted to muster a racial defense of slavery by citing Thomas Jefferson as an authoritative source. Passages from Jefferson's *Notes on the State of Virginia* were particularly popular, because they appeared to substantiate claims about the blacks' inherent inferiority. "It is not their condition," wrote Jefferson of the Negroes, "but nature, which has produced the distinction."[8] In citing Jefferson's writings these individuals paid little attention to other passages in the *Notes* that revealed the founding father's evasiveness, ambiguity and uncertainty about racial assumptions. They overlooked his acknowledgement that his thoughts about inferiority were a "suspicion only" and could be proved incorrect by "further observation."[9] Instead, they found Jefferson's theorizing about race a useful reference point for defending slavery at a time when the religon and philosophy of the day put their case in a bad light. Environmentalists showed their frustration with this use of Jefferson's ideas during the 1800 presidential election. Noting the way some writers treated the *Notes* as an anti-Negro document, one critic said of Jefferson, "You have advanced the strongest argument for their state of slavery."[10]

New economic and political developments in the country during the first two decades of the nineteenth century helped to transform attitudes about slavery and race. Eli Whitney's cotton gin made extraction of flax seed fast and inexpensive and opened the way for broad expansion of the Southern cotton belt. More and more, slaveholders looked south and west for new planting opportunities. A land boom spread until the financial panic of 1819 and then developed at an even faster pace in the 1820s and 1830s. In the meantime, talk of emancipating the slaves became less active in the South. The idealistic fervor of the Revolutionary years passed, and fear of slave revolts grew with the reports of Gabriel's plot in Virginia and the news of a major uprising in Saint-Domingue. Southerners turned increasingly anxious about the presence of free blacks in the cities, worrying that the example might inspire slaves to question their own position. Some Southern leaders pushed the idea of African colonization as a way to rid themselves of the menace of black freedmen and avoid the expected racial tensions if many whites and free Negroes lived side by side.

The Congressional debates of 1819–1820, which led to the Missouri Compromise, provided a major forum for expressing the changing views on slavery and race. Spirited arguments developed when Missouri applied for statehood as a slave state and Congressman James Tallmadge of New York introduced an amendment to prohibit the further introduction of slavery into Missouri. Thanks to the rapidly growing Northern population, Tallmadge's amendment passed in the House of Representatives in 1819. Panicked Southerners mustered their forces in the Senate and there succeeded in soundly defeating the amendment. When Congress next met, the Missouri issue came up again, and tense debates on the subject continued into 1820. After long and abrasive discussions, a compromise was worked out. Missouri came into the Union as a slave state, while Maine entered as a free state.

Confrontations in Congress over the right to extend slavery to new territory led logically to considerations of the morality of the institution itself. Many Northerners opposed slavery in Missouri primarily because they did not want white laborers to have to compete with slave labor, but the more they debated their case, the more they were tempted to speak about the rights of blacks as well as whites. Even James Tallmadge, who stressed the economic evils of slavery, peppered his speeches with references to the Declaration of Independence and the equality of all men.[11] As Jonathan Roberts of Pennsylvania noted, the concept that "all men are created equal" was the very "corner stone of our laws and our polity."[12] Mixing inspiration from the Bible and the Enlightenment, Walter Lowrie, also a Pennsylvanian, said God "hath made the world and all things therein, hath made of one blood all the nations of men." He asserted, "It is not among the natural rights of man to enslave his fellow man."[13] In even crisper language Arthur Livermore of New Hampshire said, "Justice, sir, is blind to colors, and weighs the rights of all men, whether white or black."[14]

The Southern congressmen who argued in favor of extending slavery into Missouri first tried to justify their position with familiar claims about the "evil necessity" of slavery. The institution had become deeply rooted in the South over centuries, they said, and, unfortunately, there was no choice for present leaders but to tolerate it. The problem was without obvious remedy. Practical people understood the need to accept the world as they found it and not attempt to create the unrealistic world of their dreams.[15] This appeal to pragmatism looked silly, however, when Northern congressmen exposed the contradictions. Observing that Southerners conceded slavery was evil and lamented its existence, they wondered how, at the same time, one could insist that the unfortunate institution must spread to new areas west of the Mississippi.[16]

These trappings of debate stirred some Southern congressmen to hazard a more forceful defense of slavery and an appeal to racial consciousness. Their efforts were plagued with difficulties, however, because the nation's old Revolutionary ideals could not easily be dismissed. With hesitation, uncertainty, and ambiguity evident in their arguments, extensionists tried to lessen the force of appeals to the Declaration of Independence by stressing a distinction between ideals and reality. Slavery and racial subordination were justified in the context of common practice, they suggested. Southern slavery was not, in fact, cruel; it was humane and the blacks were well-treated well-fed, and contented. As for declarations about equality, no state in the Union fully put these commitments into practice. Society needed to recognize distinctions. States denied some people the vote because of property qualifications and other standards. Indeed, if Congress wished to recast slavery according to a utopian plan, why not confer equal rights on women? Were they, too, not God's creatures, asked the extensionists?[17]

Richard M. Johnson of Kentucky, a proponent of slavery extension, worried about the new trends in Southern argumentation. The debate seemed to be moving toward extremes, he noted, but he preferred to identify the slaveholders' case closer to a middle point on matters of slavery and race. Johnson urged flexibility. Like many other congressmen, he was troubled by the Southerners' tendency to stake out a position that contrasted dramatically with the idealism of the founding fathers. Johnson observed that an "unhappy misunderstanding" had developed and that some Southerners were defending their case in a way that might be "construed into a justification of the abstract principle of slavery."[18] He also retreated from the severely negative assessments of the Negro that were emerging in Southern rhetoric. No clear evidence on the subject was available, he claimed. Philosophers offered different ideas about the origins of color groups. Some believed that all men developed from a common stock, while others thought that blacks and whites came from different ancestors. Not knowing which theory was correct, Johnson could only conclude that the joint problems of slavery and race represented major barriers to emancipation. "Till this prejudice is eradicated, or till the Ethiopian shall change his skin, his freedom is nominal in every part of the United States," Johnson concluded.[19]

The rise of a more popular, better organized, and more radical assault on slavery in the 1830s brought new challenges to the Southerners' ambiguous case for slavery. Prominent abolitionist leaders such as William Lloyd Garrison bluntly attacked contradictions in proslavery thought. "On this subject slavery I do not wish to think, or speak, or write with moderation," said Garrison. "I will not equivocate—I will not excuse. . . ."[20] With language far more stinging than the appeals of earlier crusaders against slavery, Garrison hit hard at the soft spots in Southern logic. As a strident spokesman for the rights of blacks, he accented the old environmentalist perspective through strident statements in behalf of blacks. Garrison observed that Southerners were trying to present their thesis both ways, arguing that slavery caused prejudice and that prejudice caused slavery. Through an exercise in circular logic, slaveholders believed that "the reason why the slaves are so ignorant is because they are held in bondage; the reason why they are held in bondage is because they are so ignorant!"[21]

During the 1830s, other abolitionists echoed Garrison's environmentalism to challenge the proslavery/anti-Negro position. Abolitionists realized that the Southerners' frequent references to illiteracy, unemployment, and vagrancy among free blacks represented one of the most popular arguments employed against their crusade for emancipation. Often they confronted this challenge by acknowledging the economic and social difficulties of free blacks, but they blamed the problems on slavery. Poor work habits and poor "moral" behavior were the consequence of bondage.[22] "Undoubtedly the Negros are debased," admitted William Ellery Channing, "for were slavery not debasing, I should have little quarrel with it."[23] Lydia Maria Child offered a similar environmentalist viewpoint by attributing the lying, stealing, and promiscuity associated with blacks to behavior learned under slavery. Once blacks became fully experienced in freedom, she argued, they lost these bad habits and became responsible citizens.[24] Similarly, William Jay speculated that if the South's white leaders had been raised from infancy in the same conditions as the slaves, they, too, would probably be the drones and pests of society.[25]

Cassius Clay, a former slaveholder and pugnacious politician from Kentucky, presented some of the boldest statements for environmentalism. Clay's remarks in defense of the Negro were particularly impressive, because he delivered them in a slaveholding region. Through speeches and newspaper editorials, he campaigned for emancipation in Lexington, Kentucky, drawing threats of bodily harm from angry citizens. The six-foot three-inch, 215-pound abolitionist resisted challengers with fists, a bowie knife, and a pistol. His fierce individualism won him the reputation of Kentucky's most colorful antislavery leader.

Like many other free soilers who opposed slavery's extension into the territories, Cassius Clay noted the way the slave system impoverished whites. Emphasizing the economic liabilities of slavery, he fought to create new opportunities for the whites through a free labor economy. But unlike many other prominent free soilers, Clay did not let his plea for the whites lead to neglect of the blacks. Clay denounced the stupidity of racial prejudice and tried to identify the conditions that made bigotry popular. Slavery was the primary cause of racial prejudice, he said, and emancipation would make possible its decline. "That the black man is inferior to the white, I readily allow," he said, "but that vice may depress the one, and virtue, by successive generations, elevate the other, till the two races meet on one common level, I am also firmly convinced." Where Negroes were given opportunities to improve themselves, such as in Brazil and Europe, he noted, they achieved high literary and social status. An African had the same potential for growth as a Saxon or a Frenchman. The main obstacle to reaching this potential was slavery, which left a terrible effect on white attitudes. "We made slavery," Clay concluded, "and slavery makes prejudice."[26]

The growing challenge of abolitionism, characterized by popular use of the environmentalist persuasion, forced slavery's defenders to reassess their position. Southern argumentation about slavery and race changed significantly in the 1830s and moved toward a more general defense of black bondage and racial subordination, but the transformation took time to develop. Old concepts and principles were repudiated only after long and cautious reviews of ideas long associated with the American Revolution. The 1830s were a period of transition, a time when Southern thinking moved gradually away from the equality themes of the Declaration of Independence and towards a far more conservative view of relationships between man and society.

During the 1830s, defenders of slavery frequently displayed ambiguity towards the nature/nurture controversy. While they showed interest in the idea of inherent black inferiority, often they hedged in drawing conclusions about the permanence of racial differences. Lacking prestigious support from religion, science, or national ideology to bolster their argument for racial subordination, proslavery theorists suggested that several explanations for black bondage were potentially valid. Sometimes they opposed emancipation by claiming blacks were culturally unprepared for freedom; sometimes they talked about the possibility of innate incapacity for freedom, and often they discussed combinations of the two. Their openness to a variety of workable arguments was evident in the debates of the Virginia constitutional convention of 1829-1830, when some representatives from the Old Dominion's western districts appealed for emancipation of the slaves. Speaking in defense of slavery, a delegate from Rockridge insisted that the Bill of Rights and other social compacts of the Enlightenment era were irrelevant to the emancipation controversy. There were many reasons for keeping the blacks enslaved, said the delegate, and the case for bondage did not rest on one explanation alone. One might argue that blacks did not have the capacity to become good citizens or that prejudice against them precluded good citizenship or that the great profits from Negro labor made slavery necessary. "It is perfectly immaterial what reason for excluding them may be," said the delegate, "if it is sufficient to induce us to do so."[27]

As the abolitionist challenge grew, the slaveholders' precise reason for opposing emancipation no longer seemed "immaterial." Leaders reacted not only to the rise of Garrisonian abolitionism in the North, but to threatening signs in the South as well. Nat Turner's bloody slave insurrection was followed by another effort of Virginia politicians to review the emancipation question in open debate. The discussion in the legislature was intense, and after a long fight, a motion supporting the principle of abolition legislation lost by a vote of 73 to 58. Virginia's public manifestations of doubt about slavery inspired an angry professor at the College of William and Mary to write a classic defense of slavery. In his *Review of the Debate of the Virginia Legislature of 1831 and 1832* (published in 1832), Thomas R. Dew presented most of the major arguments that would become central to the proslavery case in the years to follow. Yet on some fundamental points about the morality of slavery and racial subordination, Dew remained far less conclusive than the leading Southern polemicists of the 1840s and 1850s. He defended slavery in terms that suggested the institution was *both* an evil necessity and a positive good, and he wavered back and forth between cultural and racial reasons for opposing black emancipation.[28]

Despite his propensity for making strong negative statements about the Negro, Dew could not find authoritative evidence to support his contentions. In lieu of scientific sources he turned to lessons from history. Dew cited examples of laziness among recently freed serfs in Poland and Hungary to support his idea that America's slaves were incapable of handling freedom.[29] The reference excited a quick response from abolitionists. "These serfs were in fact *white* slaves," noted William Jay, exposing a glaring contradiction in Dew's argument.[30] If the problems of all freedmen, black and white, related to their earlier experience with servility, the racial case against emancipation seemed weak.

William Drayton, author of an important proslavery tract published in 1836, was similarly ambiguous about the nature versus nurture controversy. Like Dew, he recited a catalog of pejorative descriptions of Negroes, calling them "inert," "unintellectual," "voluptuous," and "indolent." Negroes were much better off under the paternalistic care of their masters than in freedom, he asserted.[31] But Drayton could not clearly identify the origins of the Negro's supposed deficiencies. The fundamental question remained: Did physical differences lead to prejudice, or did the conditions of slavery cause prejudice? Uncertain of the answer, Drayton tried to take a stand on slippery middle ground. Both explanations might be true, he suggested. He resisted abolition because of "nature" and "race" on the one hand and of "position" and "necessity" on the other. Drayton admitted that he could find no complete proof of the black man's inferiority, but, like Dew, he claimed that the absence of a self-sustained black civilization in Africa, the West Indies, or Haiti indicated there might be good reason for questioning the assumption of equality.[32]

By the late 1830s and early 1840s, proslavery propagandists were finding new "scientific" evidence to help them resolve contradictions in their view of Negro slavery. New theories about human differentiation were emerging from the academic disciplines of physical anthropology, physiology, and ethnology. In later decades many of these crude concepts would fall under severe attack from professional scientists. During the antebellum period, however, the spurious theories attracted a large and interested readership, and the fast growth of the new literature gave proslavery spokesmen badly needed ammunition for their forensic duels with abolitionists. As historian George M. Fredrickson points out, the efforts to raise prejudice to the level of a science gave slavery's defenders new respectibility.

Dr. Samuel George Morton, a Philadelphia physician and professor of anatomy, provided some particularly relevant evidence for the propagandists, although Morton's purpose in carrying out research was apparently to advance scientific knowledge rather than to serve the particular proslavery interests of the South. In *Crania Americana* (1839) Morton reported on his measurements of skulls from various regions of the world. He claimed his research showed that the internal capacity of the Negro's skull was, on the average, significantly smaller than the internal capacity of the Caucasian's skull.[33]

Southern leaders such as James H. Hammond and John C. Calhoun showed a keen interest in Morton's book. Above all, the Mobile, Alabama, physician Josiah Nott publicized the political implications of Morton's research for a large audience. Nott concluded from the research of Morton and others that distinctions between blacks and whites could be traced back to the origins of mankind. The two groups had developed from different species, he contended. Nott bolstered his argument with references to United States census reports that, he claimed, showed fundamental differences between white and Negro levels of criminality and insanity. Through lively magazine essays and a major book, *Types of Mankind*, Nott pressed the case for the separate origins concept.[34]

The South's initial enthusiasm for Nott flagged temporarily when some religionists took issue with the biblical implications of his theories. Nott's polygenic interpretation of man's origins directly challenged the scriptual interpretation of creation. It clashed dramatically with the story of Adam and Eve, they claimed. All mankind derived from this single biblical source, and theories to the contrary, however politically popular, could not be accepted. Throughout the 1840s and 1850s, this conflict in the South between religious and secular interpretations complicated Nott's effort to strengthen the case for permanent racial differences. Yet many proslavery propagandists found ways to sidestep the controversy and employ Nott's theories. While engaging in polemical debates with the abolitionists, they could not allow such an impressive idea to slip away from them. Frequently, they avoided reference to the science-versus-religion quarrel and concentrated instead on the political implications of the new theories.[35]

Southern propagandists approached the emancipation issue with new confidence once the "scientific" racial concepts gained fashion. The public's growing interest in biological science appeared to give them license to defend black slavery as a permanent and good institution. It helped remove the self-doubts and embarrassment associated with earlier efforts to defend slavery. In 1853 Chancellor Harper admitted that, until very recently, slaveholders typically deferred to outside judgment in discussions about Negro inferiority, but the new evidence allowed them to decide for themselves. The research of anatomists and physiologists showed that Negro inferiority derived from inherent factors and not just from "degradation produced by slavery."[36] Henry F. James cheered Dr. Morton's ground-breaking research on cranial structure, claiming that it settled "forever the relative position . . . [Negroes] occupy in the intellectual world."[37] Dr. Nott added his voice to the praise for Morton by saying the new advances in science exposed the ignorance of "the angry and senseless discussion on Negro emancipation, which have agitated Christiandom for the last half century. . . ."[38]

In the last decade before the Civil War comments about permanent racial differences were more prominent in Southern proslavery thought than ever before. The new theme, which emphasized inherent inferiority, superceded the cultural interpretation. While apologists continued to suggest that the blacks' experience in slavery made them incapable of freedom, the racial argument now appeared more firmly planted at the foundation of their defense.

With the latest word from science serving as apparent encouragement for new theorizing about racial differences, propagandists did not hesitate to add their own observations to the growing catalogue of claims about Negroes. For example, S.A. Cartwright, a medical doctor from Louisiana, insisted that measurements on the spirometer showed blacks consumed 20 percent less oxygen that whites. This difference explained the problem of "molasses blood sluggishly circulating" in the Negro's body.[39] R. R. Cobb turned to entomology for insights. Referring to the "law of nature," he claimed that red ants typically fought, captured, and subjugated "the black or Negro ants. . . ." Cobb also found supporting evidence in dermatology and phrenology. Dark skin made the Negro well-suited for his work, he assured readers, because dark pigmentation aided endurance in the hot sun. Furthermore, the Negro's supposedly small brain was functional, because it made him a submissive, obedient, and contented worker.[40]

This accumulation of damning scientific evidence made abolitionist appeals in the name of Christianity and the Enlightenment appear hopelessly idealistic, while making slavery look like a blessing for the Negro. In view of the latest "scientific evidence," freedom appeared to be a burden for blacks, and slavery seemed benign. The slave's moral character could not be improved through emancipation, said David Christy, because "The savage, liberated from bondage, is still a savage."[41] The Negro fared much better under the generous tutelage of slavery. He would never improve to a level equal to whites, but the system helped to elevate him to a higher degree of civilization. As R. R. Cobb summed up the advantages, "a state of bondage, so far from doing violence to the law of nature, develops and perfects it; and that, in that state, [the Negro] enjoys the greatest amount of happiness, and arrives of the greatest degree of perfection of which his nature is capable."[42]

This picture of good slavery for inferior Negroes nicely supported Southern concepts of paternalism. Proslavery polemicists eagerly pointed out the connection. They talked about the horrors of Africa, where many "savages" practiced cannibalism. In America blacks were protected from these outrages by the humanizing slave system. Thanks to the kind master, their needs for food, shelter, and clothing were adequately met, and they learned to work productively in a peaceful society.[43] The native African could not be degraded, said Albert Taylor Bledsoe; rather, he was improved and elevated through servitude in the United States. For such people, slavery was a blessing, freedom a curse.[44]

As documents extolling the virtues of slavery and racial subordination were disseminated widely in the South during the 1850s, some of the most enthusiastic polemicists found themselves stumbling into a corner of contradictions. The more they glorified slavery as a universal good, the less slavery appeared to be an opportunity limited only to blacks. The trouble appeared most noticeably in a controversial article featured in the Richmond *Enquirer* in 1856. An anonymous author claimed:

the South now maintains that slavery is right, natural, and necessary, and does not depend upon difference of complexion. While it is far more obvious that negroes should be slaves than whites, for they are fit to labor, not to direct, yet the principle of slavery is itself right, and *does not depend upon difference of complexion.*[45]

Abolitionists targeted the statement as a glaring example of the extremes to which an abstract defense of slavery could carry Southerners.[46] Many spokesmen for slavery, in turn, fully disclaimed interest in white bondage and attempted to stay as far away as possible from such a political bombshell. Nevertheless, the problem continued to crop up. As various proslavery writers entrapped themselves in highly complex philosophical treatises on slavery, they had to confront the obvious question: If slavery was so good, why should not some of society's troubled whites benefit from it too? Only one basic answer served to spring them quickly from the trap: a retreat into racial theory. In Albert Taylor Bledsoe's treatise, *Liberty and Slavery*, for example, the early chapters guided readers through so many abstract theories about the beauty of slavery that the black man hardly seemed at the center of the controversy. Bledsoe's principal arguments rested on the concepts of Locke, Hobbes, and

Blackstone, ideas that were used to point out the ways slavery engendered a society that best enhanced the welfare of all. Racism did not enter the analysis significantly until well into the book.[47] George Fitzhugh withheld his trump card even longer in *Cannibals All!* In the early chapters Fitzhugh contrasted capitalist exploitation of "free" laborers in England and the industrial cities of the Northern United States with the treatment of slaves on Southern plantations. While the masters' concern for their slaves was in the proprietors' best interest, argued Fitzhugh, capitalists played free laborers off against each other to force them to work for a pittance. Many "free" workers faced the horrors of unemployment, vagrancy, and the notorious poorhouses. Fitzhugh even suggested that such invidious comparisons might entice the North to consider a system of slavery. Towards the end of his analysis, however, he was forced to explain why the benign institution could not be a windfall to poor whites as well as to blacks. Fitzhugh, like Bledsoe and other proslavery propagandists, reached for the most attractive forensic weapon available under the circumstances. Mustering derogatory statements about group distinctions, Fitzhugh finished by limiting the gift of slavery to blacks because of "inferiority, or rather peculiarity, of race. . . ."[48]

By the eve of the Civil War, Southern proslavery thought and anti-Negro thought had changed considerably from the rather loose and ambivalent position of the Revolutionary period. The Southerners' efforts to defend their way of life had hardened into stiff proclamations about the "positive good" of slavery. Almost parallel to these changes came bolder, unabashed claims about white superiority and black inferiority. These changes in Southern thought took a long time to take effect. The transformations developed slowly at first but gained momentum as the abolitionist campaign in the North emerged in force. Abolitionism provoked slaveholders into sharpening their rationale for the peculiar institution. As debates over slavery turned more intense, it became evident to many Southerners that a positive justification of slavery was unpersuasive without a strong racial component. The confrontation called for a defense of slavery based on references to black inequality, an argument that developed into one of the South's most fundamental appeals against emancipation.

Notes

1. Dwight L. Dumond, ed., *Letters of James Gillespie Birney*, 2 vols. (New York, 1938), 1:224.

2. For a general discussion of this subject, see George M. Fredrickson, *The Black Image in the White Mind: The Debate on Afro-American Character and Destiny, 1817-1914* (New York, 1971); William Stanton, *The Leopard's Spots: Scientific Attitudes Toward Race in America, 1815-59* (Chicago, 1960).

3. John Chester Miller, *The Wolf by the Ears: Thomas Jefferson and Slavery* (New York, 1977), pp. 55-56; William Sumner Jenkins, *Pro-Slavery Thought in the Old South* (Chapel Hill, 1935), pp. 34-35, 44, 52; Winthrop D. Jordan, *White Over Black: American Attitudes Toward the Negro, 1550-1812* (Baltimore, 1969), pp. 306, 308, 326, 447-48; Don B. Kates, Jr., "Abolition, Deportation, Integration: Attitudes Toward Slavery in the Early Republic," *Journal of Negro History* (January 1968), p. 33; Stanton, *The Leopard's Spots*, pp. 2, 9, 15, 18.

4. Jordan, *White Over Black*, pp. 275, 282-89.

5. Samuel Stanhope Smith, *An Essay on the Causes of the Variety of Complexion and Figure in the Human Species* (Philadelphia, 1787), pp. 10-24, 39-40, 57-60.

6. Jenkins, *Pro-Slavery Thought*, pp. 34-35; David Brion Davis, *The Problem of Slavery in the Age of Revolution, 1770-1823* (Ithaca, 1975), p. 169.

7. Davis, *The Problem of Slavery in the Age of Revolution*, pp. 85-87, 255-57, 262, (quotation, pp. 299-300); Robert McColley, *Slavery and Jeffersonian Virginia* (Urbana, 1964), pp. 2, 87, 120, 124, 189.

8. Thomas Jefferson, *Notes on the State of Virginia*, ed. William Pedden (Chapel Hill, 1955), pp. 138-43.

9. Ibid., pp. 142-43.

10. Stanton, *The Leopard's Spots*, pp. 18, (quotation, 55).

11. *Annals of Congress*, House of Representatives, 15th Cong. (1819), vol. 1, p. 1211.

12. *Annals of Congress*, U.S. Senate, 16th Cong., 1st sess. (1820), pp. 123-26.

13. Ibid., p. 201.

14. *Annals of Congress*, House of Representatives, 15th Cong. (1819), vol. 1, p. 1192.

15. *Annals of Congress*, U.S. Senate, 16th Cong., 1st sess. (1820), pp. 131-32, 138, 437-48, 401.

16. Ibid., p. 207.

17. Ibid., pp. 173, 350-51, 394, 412-13.

18. Ibid., p. 345.

19. Ibid., pp. 357–58.

20. *The Liberator*, vol. 1, January 1, 1831.

21. William Lloyd Garrison, *Thoughts on African Colonization* (Boston, 1832), p. 86.

22. Ronald G. Walters, *The Antislavery Appeal: American Abolitionism after 1830* (Baltimore, 1976), pp. 64–68.

23. William E. Channing, *Emancipation* (Boston, 1840), p. 63.

24. Duberman, ed., *The Antislavery Vanguard*, pp. 172–73; Lydia Maria Francis Child, *An Appeal in Favor of That Class of Americans Called Africans* (New York, 1836), p. 134–35, 171, 175.

25. Quoted in John L. Thomas, ed., *Slavery Attacked: The Abolitionist Crusade* (Englewood Cliffs, N.J., 1965), p. 22.

26. Horace Greeley, ed., *The Writings of Cassius Marcellus Clay, Including Speeches and Addresses* (New York, 1848), pp. 93–94, 193, 199, 206, 231.

27. *Proceedings and Debates of the Virginia State Convention of 1829–1830* (Richmond, 1830), pp. 225–26.

28. Thomas R. Dew, *Review of the Debate in the Virginia Legislature of 1831 and 1832* (Richmond, 1832), pp. 5, 12–13, 39, 52, 87–89, 106–107.

29. Ibid., p. 97.

30. *Slavery Attacked*, p. 22.

31. William Drayton, *The South Vindicated from the Treason and Fanaticism of the Northern Abolitionists* (Philadelphia, 1836), pp. 69, 81, 230, 232.

32. Ibid., pp. 19, 43, 80–86, 112, 115, 117.

33. Samuel George Morton, *Crania Americana; or, A Comparative View of the Skulls of Various Aboriginal Nations of North and South America, to Which is Prefixed an Essay on the Varieties of the Human Species* (Philadelphia, 1839).

34. Josiah Nott, *Types of Mankind: or, Ethnological Researches, Based upon the Ancient Monuments, Paintings, Sculptures, and Crania of Races, and upon Their National, Geographical, Philological and Biblical History. . .* (Philadelphia, 1854).

35. Stanton, *The Leopard's Spots*, pp. 122–23, 194.

36. Chancellor Harper, "Memoir on Slavery," in *The Pro-Slavery Argument, As Maintained by the Most Distinguished Writers of the Southern States* (Philadelphia, 1853), pp. 58–59.

37. [Henry F. James], *Abolitionism Unveiled! Hypocrisy Unmasked! and Knavery Scourged! . . .* (New York, 1850), p. 11.

38. Stanton, *The Leopard's Spots*, p. 81.

39. S. A. Cartwright, "Slavery in the Light of Ethnology," in E. N. Elliott,

ed., *Cotton Is King and Proslavery Arguments* (Augusta, Ga., 1860), pp. 695, 705.

40. R. R. Cobb, *An Inquiry into the Law of Negro Slavery in the United States of America* (Philadelphia, 1858), vol. 2, pp. 8, 23–24, 27–29, 32–42.

41. David Christy, "Cotton Is King, or Slavery in the Light of Political Economy," in *Cotton Is King,* p. 42.

42. Cobb, *An Inquiry into the Law of Negro Slavery,* pp. 51–52.

43. James Williams, *Letters on Slavery from the Old World* (Middle District of Tennessee, 1861), pp. 17, 22–23, 32; Edward Pollard, *Black Diamonds, Gathered in the Darkey Homes of the South* (New York, 1859), pp. 45, 81; William Gilmore Simms, "The Morals of Slavery," in *The Pro-Slavery Argument,* pp. 262, 270. 273–74; "Speech of the Hon. H. S. Foote of Mississippi," *De Bow's Review* (August 1859), p. 219.

44. Albert Taylor Blesdoe, "Liberty and Slavery: or, Slavery in the Light of Moral and Political Philosophy," in *Cotton Is King,* p. 303.

45. Quoted in Russel B. Nye, *Fettered Freedom: Civil Liberties and the Slavery Controversy, 1830–1860* (East Lansing, Mich. 1949), p. 238.

46. Charles Sumner, *The Barbarism of Slavery: Speech of Hon. Charles Sumner on the Bill for the Admission of Kansas as a Free State, in the U.S. Senate, June 4, 1860* (Washington, D.C., 1860), p. 27.

47. Blesdoe, "Liberty and Slavery," pp. 275–79, 288, 295–96, 311, 335–38.

48. George Fitzhugh, *Cannibals All!, or Slaves Without Masters,* ed. C. Vann Woodward (Cambridge, Mass., 1960), pp. 6–9, 15–16, 25– 29, 77, 187, 201. Also, *see* the discussion in Eugene D. Genovese, *The World the Slaveholders Made: Two Essays in Interpretation* (New York, 1969), pp. 118, 129, 208, 235–36, 238.

Between Black and White: Attitudes Toward Southern Mulattoes, 1830-1861*

The mulatto was a casualty of the hardening attitudes toward slavery and race. Before the crisis of abolitionism, Americans from both North and South openly expressed a marked bias favoring the mulatto over the Negro, and often they gave mulattoes preferential treatment. Although the special opportunities given to American mulattoes were never as attractive as in Brazil, where a mulatto escape hatch allowed many lightskins to approach the status of whites, the distinctions were nevertheless significant. Why, then, did the likeness to a second-tier position for mulattoes begin to fade away as the South moved toward the Civil War?

The documents of slavery—laws, narratives, speeches, and political tracts—contain abundant references to "Negroes" and "mulattoes."[1] By the standards of antebellum America, the distinction was not accidental or minor. Contemporary attitudes about the difference between Negro and mulatto related to fundamental racial ideas. Variations in white attitudes toward mulattoes in the antebellum period need closer investigation than they have received, especially in connection with conflicting opinions about miscegenation, sexual oppression, and racial identification. In many respects disputes about

*The original version of "Between Black and White: Attitudes Toward Southern Mulattoes, 1830-1861" by the author appeared in *Journal of Southern History,* vol. 45, no. 2 (May 1979), pp. 185-200. Copyright 1979 by the Southern Historical Association. Reprinted in revised form by permission of the managing editor.

the mulatto's position in southern society related to fundamental points in the debates about slavery and abolition.

Historians of slavery recognize that antebellum Americans often showed special interest in mulattoes, but their estimates of the extent and importance of this interest vary greatly. In a careful study of white attitudes from 1550 to 1812 Winthrop D. Jordan notes that the term mulatto was used far less frequently in the early development of North America than in the Spanish and French settlements and even the English colonies of the Caribbean. Jordan concludes that "mulattoes [in North America] do not seem to have been accorded higher status than Negroes in actual practice."[2]

Focusing on the nineteenth century in *Roll, Jordan, Roll*, Eugene D. Genovese suggests that the South's mulattoes were more numerous than officially reported in the census returns, and he shows that some mulatto house servants, urban slaves, and freedmen exhibited snobbery toward the darker Negroes. But Genovese sees the South's two-part, white-black racial system as a formidable obstacle to the mulattoes' class aspirations. Whites usually considered a mulatto to be "just another nigger" and, consequently, "drove the mulattoes into the arms of the blacks, no matter how hard some tried to build a make-believe third world for themselves."[3] Robert William Fogel and Stanley L. Engerman are less critical of the census reports in *Time on the Cross*. Observing that mulattoes represented only 7.7 percent of the slaves in 1850 and 10.4 percent in 1860, they attribute earlier estimates of a large mulatto population to impressionable travelers in the South. These visitors spent most of their time in the cities, where mulattoes were concentrated, Fogel and Engerman maintain; and the travelers did not get adequate firsthand knowledge of conditions in the countryside, where Negroes made up 95 percent of the slave population. Fogel and Engerman also give little attention to reports of preferential treatment for mulattoes.[4]

Carl N. Degler's excellent comparative study, *Neither Black nor White*, is particularly relevant to an examination of attitudes toward the mulatto. Degler observes that in Brazil mulattoes were important both in terms of numbers and social privileges but that this pattern did not develop in the United States. Degler carefully identifies judicial rulings of the slavery period that show some Americans wanted to give mulattoes favored treatment over Negroes, but he finds these cases very irregular and not representative of the prevailing view. Discussing the implications for modern times, he says, "There are only two qualities in the United States racial pattern: black and white. A person is one or the other; there is no intermediate position."[5]

Whether the mulattoes' place was considered significantly distinct in antebellum America depends partly on the way contemporaries labeled them in the population data. Authorities did list mulattoes separately from Negroes in the census reports on slaves and free blacks. Nevertheless, it is not possible to provide a confident estimate of the size of the mulatto population during this period because estimates were highly subjective. Census marshals did not receive adequate instructions for careful judgment, and they did not have common criteria for distinguishing Negroes from mulattoes.[6] The 1860 census reported that mulattoes represented 10.4 percent of the slave population and 36.2 percent of the free black population (31.0 percent in the Northern states, 40.8 percent in the Southern), but these figures had a great margin of error.[7] During the antebellum period abolitionists and slavocrats argued about the "true" number of mulattoes, since a large population of "mixed-bloods" could be interpreted as evidence of widespread miscegenation under slavery. In the 1850s Senator Thomas Lanier Clingman of North Carolina wrote to the census board, asking that it help to resolve the dispute by recording more accurate information. The author of an article in *De Bow's Review*, describing Clingman's letter, wrote that the 1850 "census was notoriously faulty in this respect [and, consequently] . . . nothing like a true knowledge of the state of the black race in the United States has been arrived at."[8]

Travelers' accounts from the period make the mulatto population appear more substantial in certain regions of the country than the census figures suggest. Alexis de Tocqueville observed after his visit in 1831 and 1832 that, "In some parts of America, the European and the negro races are so crossed by one another that it is rare to meet with a man who is entirely black, or entirely white . . . ."[9] Harriet Martineau, the English visitor who also traveled through the United States in the 1830s, expressed great interest in signs of miscegenation in the South, including the presence of very light-skinned mulattoes among the leading families of Louisiana.[10] Yankee traveler Frederick

Law Olmsted displayed curiosity, too. Surprised to find so "many fine-looking mulattoes, and nearly white colored persons . . .," he wrote, "The majority of those with whom I have come personally in contact with are such."[11]

These accounts, while revealing that mulattoes occupied prominent positions in the South, do not necessarily indicate that miscegenation was prevalent throughout the area. Fogel and Engerman's warning about unrepresentative groupings in the cities is pertinent. Many travelers developed their impressions from sojourns in such favorite tourist spots in the South as Charleston and New Orleans. These cities contained a far greater proportion of mulatto slaves and freedmen than most plantation districts. Tocqueville tried to put this matter into perspective by noting that the number of Americans of mixed ancestry was greater than a visitor might first expect but that it was much smaller than the proportion of mulattoes in other regions of the western hemisphere.[12]

The mulattoes' significance in antebellum life relates not to their numbers but to the special attention society gave to them. The presence of mulattoes reminded all parties in the debates over slavery that miscegenation was a reality in Southern life and that most white-black sexual unions developed out of master-slave relationships. Disputes about the number of mulattoes thus related to larger questions about the oppressiveness of slavery. Attitudes toward mulattoes also reflected some of the subtle racial biases of the times. Many Southern whites preferred mulattoes to darker Negroes and provided them with better opportunities in slavery and in freedom. By the late antebellum period society's promulatto bias appeared to be a tactical advantage for abolitionists in their campaigns against slavery, a situation that forced the defenders of slavery to reconsider their tendency to distinguish mulattoes from Negroes.

The issue of white-black sexual relations under slavery became highly volatile in the antebellum years, and mulattoes were at the center of the controversy. The mulattoes' very existence served to highlight the reality of miscegenation. Abolitionists considered the South's mulatto population living proof of one of the fundamental "moral" issues of slavery: the sexual promiscuity of white males and the sexual oppression of black women. Furthermore, the abolitionists asserted, the behavior that produced mulattoes tore at the marriage bonds of both groups. The temptations reportedly led whites to neglect and dishonor their wives while seeking relationships in the slave quarters.[13] These intrusions in turn undermined the institution of marriage among the slaves. Abolitionists predicted that the rampant licentiousness in Southern society, evidenced by mulatto offspring, would pass with the end of slavery.

Accusations of sexual promiscuity drew strong public reaction in mid-nineteenth-century America, and antislavery leaders did not miss the opportunity to make political capital out of the issue. They particularly enjoyed commenting on a Southerner's unguarded confession that "the best blood of Virginia flows in the veins of the slaves." Charles Sumner used the quotation in a blistering speech against the South, and Charles Grandison Parsons noted that the miscegenation implied in the statement was "not less true of the other slave States."[14] David Lee Child also referred to the statement, complaining that slaveholders could not give up their "habits of roving desire." That miscegenation "prevails to a most shameful extent, is proved from the rapid increase of mulattoes," Child asserted.[15]

Abolitionists considered this evidence of the slaveholders' promiscuity a potent answer to charges that emancipation could lead to widespread sexual contact and "amalgamation" of the races. "Southern amalgamation" under slavery was already a reality, they said, because slavery was primarily responsible for expanding the mulatto population in America.[16] "If gentlemen wish to see where this evil prevails," said Abram Pryne, "Let them look at the variegated colors in the South."[17] William Lloyd Garrison also exploited the irony. When a slaveholder asked him the familiar question, "'How should you like to have a black man marry your daughter?' Garrison replied that 'Slaveholders generally should be the last persons to affect fastidiousness on that point, for they seem to be enamoured of amalgamation.'"[18]

Abolitionists eagerly publicized reports about slave concubines in the South. They cited familiar stories concerning lightskinned mistresses who served as regular partners to Southern whites, and they showed particular interest in the quadroon balls of New Orleans, where gentlemen arranged liaisons with beautiful women. Abolitionists likened the mistresses to expensive prostitutes, but there was an important difference in the slaves' case: these "prostitutes" were involuntary paramours. They were not free to give up their profession. Abolitionist propaganda contained many reports on the rearing of young mulatto girls for forced sale as concubines. They reminded readers that the pretty ones commanded high prices on the slave market for sordid reasons.[19] As an anonymous writer recalled, in an auction of "nigger wenches" slave traders unabashedly presented the victims as "warranted virgins," excellent as potential concubines, and valuable for "the manufacture of light colored slaves."[20]

These commentaries on licentiousness under slavery also appeared in popular literature. Antislavery novels developed a subtle form of racial appeal. They encouraged readers to identify with slave heroines by describing them as whitelike in appearance and manners. As Jules Zanger has shown, the "Tragic Octoroon" often figured as a central character in antislavery fiction. The octoroon (seven-eighths white by ancestry) appeared as a beautiful young woman with only the slightest evidence of Negro forebears. In the familiar plot she grew up in her white father's household and received a good education, but her father's death led to a chain of tragedies: sale into slavery and victimization at the hands of a cruel and lustful slave trader or overseer. Readers were outraged by the sexual abuses committed against these fictional octoroons, identifying emotionally with the nearly white characters who suffered the double crimes of slavery and rape.[21]

Proslavery writers responded to attacks against the "morals of slavery" with confusion and uncertainty. They could not decide whether to denounce the accusations of promiscuity or to rationalize the situation. On the one hand, some dismissed the charges as unfair and inaccurate. Mulattoes made up only a small proportion of the Negro population, they said. It was their presence in cities and towns that led Yankee and foreign visitors to exaggerate grossly the extent of miscegenation. Southern society did not easily tolerate liaisons with slave women, they said, and a gentleman known for such escapades could lose face in his community.[22] On the other hand, many defenders of slavery could not easily deny the prevalence of white-black sexual contacts or the relaxed attitudes many Southern males showed toward them. Proslavery writers tried to answer poignant comments about immorality with more than just evasion or denial; sometimes they sought to excuse the behavior.

Some proslavery figures, especially South Carolinians, openly defended the relationships with slave women. James Henry Hammond berated "learned old maids like Miss Martineau" who failed to understand the nature of human passions, and he denounced moralistic attacks "by Clergymen and Virgins."[23] Chancellor William Harper explained that master-slave liaisons usually involved either hot-blooded white youths, whose small resistance to temptation was understandable, or respectable gentlemen who had only casual, not habitual, encounters. It appeared much better for these men to have their flings with a slave woman than to suffer the degradation associated with meeting a white prostitute. "The colored prostitute is, in fact, a far less contaminated and depraved being," said Harper.[24] Just as these relationships seemed to protect the honor of white males, they could also be viewed as a means to protect the virtue of white females. The writers asserted that the availability of slave women for illicit affairs made rendezvous with white women less common in the South than elsewhere. William Gilmore Simms, who defended the sexual liaisons in strong terms, observed that "The negro and the colored woman in the South, supply the place, which at the north is usually filled with factory and serving girls."[25]

Some defenders of slavery excused white-black sexual contacts by praising the mulatto offspring of these relationships. They described the partly white children as a better breed than the mother. Mulattoes were a "superior race" that was "*elevated* by the mixture of blood," said Thomas Reade Rootes Cobb of Georgia. He blamed miscegenation on the "natural lewdness" of the Negro but found the problem mitigated because "Her sin does not entail misfortune but good fortune on her children." Race mixture seemed to have its benefits.[26] A Virginian believed, for example, that Negroes were more intelligent in Louisiana, in part "because the amalgamation of the races was much greater" there.[27] William Gilmore Simms appraised the problem in particularly bold language. He considered amalgamation to be perhaps a hopeful prospect that could ultimately help the South to overcome the problems of race prejudice. "The result of illicit intercourse between the differing races, is the production of a fine specimen of physical manhood, and of a better mental organization, in the mulatto; and, in the progress of a few generations, that, which might otherwise forever prove a separating wall between the white and black—the color of the later,—will be effectively removed. When the eye ceases to be offended, the mind of the white will no longer be jealous. . . ."[28]

The comments of Cobb, Simms, and others reveal a popular promulatto bias that affected the whites' day-to-day relationships with mulattoes. Many whites considered mulattoes to be superior to the darker Negroes and gave them favored treatment. The record of special treatment is well documented. Proprietors generally preferred mulattoes as house servants and plantation tradesmen and gave them more opportunities to acquire skills for these occupations than they gave the other slaves. More often than dark-skinned bondsmen, mulattoes were provided some education, enjoyed good food, clothing, and shelter, and had opportunities to move about both inside and outside the plantation.[29] Sometimes they had as much authority as plantation managers. For example, Olmsted was deeply impressed with the responsibilities of a mulatto watchman on a large rice plantation. The watchman worked as steward over several slave mechanics and carried keys to the storehouses strapped to his waist. He rationed out provisions to the white overseer as well as to the slaves. To all appearances his authority on the plantation was superior to that of the overseer.[30]

Mulattoes were very conspicuous beneficiaries of manumission. Masters often granted such freedom in order to emancipate their own children.[31] South Carolina novelist William Gilmore Simms believed that "the greater number of the southern mulattoes have been made free in consequence of their relationship to their owners."[32] Some masters lavished preferential treatment upon their slave children but preferred a minimum of publicity when providing freedom papers, either fearing community gossip about their parental relationships or interference from the state laws that prohibited manumission. Frederick Douglass recalled the case of William Wilks, whose white father allowed him such freedom of movement that he hardly seemed a slave. When Wilks became an adult, he outbid all purchasers and bought his own freedom, apparently with the help of his father.[33] Other masters acknowledged their relationship more openly. A Virginia planter, Ralph Quarles, made great efforts to ensure the future comfort of his progeny. He freed his four mulatto slave children and provided for his sons' education in Ohio. When one of his daughters married a slave, he purchased the son-in-law's freedom and gave the newlyweds a plantation and slaves. Quarles died in 1834 and left his property to his mulatto sons.[34]

Many pampered mulattoes reacted to white attitudes by considering themselves superior to the other slaves. Servants in the "Big House," who became familiar with the language and manners of the plantation owners, often looked condescendingly on the field hands.[35] These favored mulattoes "constitute the aristocracy and chivalry of the slave population of the South," said Reverend John Dixon Long.[36] Tocqueville commented on mulatto attitudes with a note of disgust. They became haughty and maintained distance from their black brothers, he noted, and when racial conflicts arose the mulattoes "generally side with the whites, just as the lackeys of the great, in Europe assume the contemptuous airs of nobility to the lower orders."[37] Color prejudice carried over to the free mulatto population as well. Lightskinned freedmen formed such exclusive clubs as the Brown Fellowship Society in Charleston and proscribed social intercourse and marriage with darkskinned blacks. Free Negroes in Charleston responded to the color snobbery by organizing the Society of Free Dark Men.[38] The pride of mulattoes affected their relationships with lower-class whites, too. Whether slave or free, mulattoes showed contempt for the poor uneducated whites.

Mulatto snobbery was, to a considerable degree, a reflection of white attitudes. Whites frequently made invidious comparisons between Negroes and mulattoes and claimed that the admixture of white blood gave mulattoes special qualities. The "pure African," as represented by the field hands, was incapable of refinement and advance, said an anonymous writer. Masters chose mulattoes for household duties because the "mixed race" was more susceptible to improvement and could handle tasks requiring higher capabilities.[39] Edwin Clifford Holland of South Carolina applied the comparison to free blacks as well. He described darkskinned blacks as "'an idle, lazy, insolent set of vagabonds, who lived by theft or gambling' . . . , [but] free mulattoes . . . [by contrast, were] 'industrious, sober, hard-working mechanics, who have large families and considerable property.'"[40] Dr. T. D. English also deprecated the capabilities of darkskinned blacks but cited the progress of mulattoes as leaders in Liberian communities and occupational climbers in the United States. He believed mulattoes possessed more "intellectual force" than Negroes and attributed the "smartness" to Caucasian admixture.[41]

While praise for mulattoes helped slaveholders to excuse and rationalize miscegenation in the South, they discovered that the Northerners' predilections for mulattoes tended to complicate the task of defending slavery. Abolitionists exploited popular Northern impressions of mulatto superiority to make a powerful emotional appeal on behalf of the slaves. By describing the slaves as whitelike in appearance and personality, they more easily stirred white audiences to relate to the victims' condition and respond with a sense of emotional outrage.

Antislavery documents contain abundant references to the supposed physical attractiveness and high intelligence of mulattoes. Appealing portraits of "handsome little mulatto boys" and "beautiful quadroon" girls appeared frequently in travelers' accounts. Frederick Law Olmsted, for example, commented on the charm, intelligence, ingenuity, and beauty of the mulattoes he encountered; and the the Reverend Philo Tower spoke glowingly of mulatto girls "of all complexions, from the light flaxen hair and bright blue eye, and the sandy and freckled countenance, and the keen, black, piercing eye, and clear, beautiful white skin, with rosy cheeks, making the very perfection of loveliness and beauty."[42] Some observers, such as Charles G. Parsons, associated their impressions with a theory of race. Mulattoes were "the best specimens of manhood to be found in the South," he said. "The African mothers have given them a good physical system, and the Anglo-Saxon fathers a good mental constitution." If mulattoes could be given one of the Carolinas to manage, thought Parsons, within a short time they could show the slaves how to take care of themselves.[43]

More than any other writer, Harriet Beecher Stowe succeeded in exploiting promulatto bias as a device for leveling a powerful indictment against slavery. Her immensely popular novel, *Uncle Tom's Cabin*, featured mulattoes as the appealing protagonists. Most of Stowe's heroes and heroines were nearly white in appearance, and she assigned them the greatest imagination, intelligence, and rebelliousness toward slavery. Eliza, the character who dared to run towards freedom across the Ohio River ice, was described as a quadroon woman of "finely moulded shape." Her son, the lightskinned Jim Crow, appeared "remarkably beautiful and engaging." Eliza's husband was "a bright and talented young mulatto" named George Harris, whose intelligence showed in the invention of a machine to clean hemp. Harris burned with desire to escape to Canada. Stowe described his father as the scion of one of Kentucky's proudest families. Related comments about mulatto characters appeared throughout the book—references to "bright-eyed mulatto" boys and lightskinned slave women whose "particular gift" was to display "beauty of a most dazzling kind."[44]

Fascination with the theme of mulatto rebelliousness, which characterized Stowe's novel, greatly interested both abolitionists and slaveholders. Various antislavery novelists portrayed dark-skinned blacks like Uncle Tom as patient, loyal, obedient, and docile but showed mulattoes as impatient and angry and some-times prone to revolt in their seething desire to break the chains of slavery.[45] "If ever the San Domingo hour comes," Stowe warned through Augustine St. Clare, "Anglo Saxon blood will lead on the day. Sons of white fathers, with all our haughty feelings burning in their veins, will not always be bought and sold and traded."[46] Stowe put her finger on a subject that had given slaveholders night-mares for many years. They had worried about the danger of al-lowing preferred treatment to buoy the self-confidence of mulattoes excessively.[47] Pampering could make them appear to be the elite of the slave community and encourage them to assume leadership in the event of a servile insurrection. Growing concerns about policing the free-black population partly reflected this belief. It appeared that the freedmen, with many mulattoes among them, could prove a particularly mischievous group.[48]

Yet slave proprietors also realized that mulatto confidence could work to their benefit. Elitist-minded mulattoes, who looked con-descendingly on the black masses in slavery and believed they enjoyed a special relationship with the white master class, could prove invaluable in a time of crisis. They might serve as valuable informants against plots for rebellion. Some slaveholders believed that the failure of the Denmark Vesey conspiracy of 1822 showed the truth of this expectation, because mulatto servants reported to their masters the plans for revolt before they could be put into effect.[49]

Generally, slaveholder opinion remained divided about the mulattoes' potential role in a crisis. Some viewed their feelings of superiority and independence as a dangerous sign; others believed the sense of superiority would make them loyal and trusted friends of the white man.

As the political controversy over abolitionism became increasingly volatile in the 1840s and 1850s, defenders of slavery found that their ambivalent attitudes toward the mulatto put them in a dilemma. Like many Northerners, they exhibited the popular prejudices of their day and judged mulattoes to be superior to Negroes, though inferior to whites. They preferred to keep the light-complexioned slaves in skilled or servant positions, and not a few considered mulatto women attractive sexual partners. In short, they could not easily overcome their promulatto bias. But these prejudices threatened to undermine their racial defense of slavery. To accept the notion that degrees of white admixture related to degrees of superiority suggested that light mulattoes, especially quadroon and octoroons, were almost as eligible for freedom as whites. The tolerance for mulattoes left slaveholders with a weak defense against certain abolitionist attacks. It gave them little to say to abolitionists who fired up emotions by focusing on the plight of the almost-white slaves. The promulatto, proslavery advocates badly needed a theory to help them squirm out of the intellectual trap into which they had fallen.

In response to this problem, Dr. Josiah Clark Nott, prominent medical doctor from Mobile, Alabama, offered a partial answer that attracted considerable interest in the slave South: the theory of hybridity. In 1842 Nott came across an anonymous letter to the *Boston Medical and Surgical Journal* that suggested a way of condemning "amalgamation" but did not conflict totally with popular preferences favoring the mulatto. The letter made mulattoes appear to be a weak freak of nature without denying their supposed mental qualities. Basing his interpretation on the writer's analysis of census data, Nott argued that mulattoes were the shortest-lived group of humans. They were less capable of enduring fatigue, exposure, and hardship than Negroes or whites, he reported, and their children died at an early age. Mulatto women were especially delicate, highly susceptible to disease, and poor breeders and nurses. Moreover, Nott accepted the writer's assumption that the mortality rate for free mulattoes was much higher than for slaves generally. Through various essays in the 1840s and 1850s, Nott developed and expanded this interpretation to argue that scientific evidence proved mulattoes were particularly fragile.[50]

Theories about mulatto sterility especially interested Nott. By considering blacks and whites distinct species he could describe the mulattoes as a "hybrid," as an "unnatural offspring, doomed by nature to work out its own destruction." Between the second and fifth generations mulattoes would allegedly become sterile (over the years he varied the number of generations estimated for extinction). This condition could be likened to a horse and an ass producing sterile mule offspring, Nott explained. There were some exceptions, of course. Recognizing that his rule of infertility could not apply inflexibly to humans, since some mulatto families had continued breeding for many generations in coastal cities such as New Orleans and Mobile, Nott theorized that some stocks were more prolific than Northern mulattoes.[51]

While Nott made mulattoes look degenerate when arguing his pseudoscientific theories about group differences, he could also make mulattoes look very attractive as individuals. Like many other white commentators of his age, Nott considered mulattoes mentally and aesthetically superior to darkskinned Negroes. They were "well formed, more robust and hardy, and their features often regular and handsome," he noted. Claiming "there is no doubt that the intellectual grade of the negro races may be greatly improved by crossing them with the whites . . . ," Nott assumed that "mulattoes . . .[were] intermediate in intelligence between the blacks and whites." Nott's condemnation of mulattoes rested mainly on a pessimistic prediction about their future rather than a rigid judgment about their mental or aesthetic inferiority in the present.[52]

It is important to note that some defenders of slavery rejected Nott's argument because they believed his theories about the multiple origins of black and white races represented an attack on orthodox religion. Nott's views on two distinct species appeared to blaspheme the scriptural account of creation and weaken the biblical defense of slavery. But many southerners did not share this attitude. Skirting the potential conflicts with religious orthodoxy, they treated Nott's interpretation as a helpful aid from "science" in the complex debate over the mulatto's condition.[53]

Not surprisingly, the "scientific" assault on mulattoes led some commentators to deny preferences for the mulatto altogether. The arguments of John H. Van Evrie reflected the growing trend toward rigidity on racial issues that would become more prominent in the postwar years. Van Evrie, a medical doctor, a northerner, and a defender of slavery, denied middle ground to mulattoes and stressed a white-black perspective on race relations.

Van Evrie considered white attitudes toward mulattoes a crucial issue in the entire antislavery debate. ". . . mulattoism is a subject of stupendous importance in itself," he said, "and as the public are generally, and the 'anti-slavery' writers especially, profoundly ignorant of it, and of all the laws that govern it, it is proposed to present the elementary principles or basis on which the whole subject rests." Van Evrie argued that abolitionists had stretched their reports of extensive amalgamation in the South far beyond reality. Mixed-bloods were not to be significant in the South's future, he insisted; rather, they would die out. "Mulattoism is an abnormalism—a disease . . .," he said, and the scientific rules of hybridity left them "mercifully doomed to final extinction." Abolitionists also had commented far too much about mulatto superiority, thought Van Evrie. The novels about beautiful "mongrel" women and reports on intelligent mulatto editors could not reverse fundamental truths. "Some mules are doubtless superior to some horses, but no mule was ever equal to the average horse; and doubtless some mulattoes have been superior to some white men, but no mulatto ever did nor ever can reach the intellectual standard of the Caucasian," Van Evrie argued. Disputing popular promulatto stereotypes, he described mulatto males as typically lazy or criminal and mulatto women as typically lewd and immoral.[54]

The views of Josiah Clark Nott, J. H. Van Evrie, and other theorists who connected hybridity and sterility attracted many debaters.[55] The subject excited interest because proslavery theorists saw it as a useful "scientific" fact to counter the attacks of abolitionists. For some, theories about hybridity provided a way to pity mulattoes without negating popular opinions about their superiority over Negroes. For others, the theories served to deny preferences for mulattoes altogether. The concept of hybridity also supported the effort to strengthen white resistance to amalgamation. Defenders of slavery considered the question of mulattoism crucial to the debate about emancipation, for if lightskinned mulattoes were to be judged almost white biologically and culturally, then the case for their near readiness for freedom could easily be advanced. Once quadroons and octoroons were deemed eligible and mentally qualified for liberty, the case for other, darker mulattoes might also be presented. Before long, this flexibility on racial matters could open a floodgate of appeals on behalf of various mixed-bloods. The American system of racial slavery could not tolerate such a sliding scale of color prejudice. It called for a more rigid, white-black pattern of social arrangements. By 1861 the dichotomy described by Carl N. Degler had become far more characteristic of American racial identification than in earlier times.

The pressures of the Civil War, Reconstruction, and the era of segregation effectively pushed the word mulatto further toward the margins of the national vocabulary. In the spring of 1861 Alexander Hamilton Stephens gave his famous "cornerstone" speech, arguing that Southern society rested on the central "truth" of inequality of the races. Stephens allowed no middle ground for mulattoes in drawing the line. The formal pattern held. Over the next century racial division indeed seemed the central theme of Southern history, and formal race doctrine did not provide a special place for mixed-bloods.[56] The slightest known Negro ancestry usually defined a person as a black, and "passing" came to mean complete identification as a white person. The behavioral patterns associated with promulatto bias persisted in day-to-day life. Subtly, informally, casually, favoritism toward lightskinned Negroes continued into modern times. From preferential hiring practices to the appearance of light-complexioned individuals among the black political and economic leadership, the evidence of persistent advantages for mulattoes remained. The complex patterns of color prejudice that developed during the years of slavery would not easily pass away.

Notes

1. The terms used to distinguish color groupings in the antebellum period varied. Some individuals distinguished between "Negroes" and "mulattoes"; others spoke of "blacks" and "mulattoes." Some writers capitalized the words black, Negro, and white, while others did not. For purposes of consistency my references in this essay will use the most familiar present-day forms: "Negro" and "mulatto." I use these words to distinguish between dark-complexioned individuals of predominately African ancestry (Negroes) and medium- and light-complexioned individuals of mixed white and black ancestry (mulattoes). It is important to remember that nineteenth-century figures usually distinguished between the two groups on the basis of personal perception rather than from a precise knowledge of ancestry. Judgments could vary greatly. For example, some described a person of medium complexion as mulatto, while others considered the person a Negro. We should also remember that antebellum terminology was complicated further by the tendency of many writers to use Negro or black as a generic term to describe all individuals with identifiable African ancestry.

2. Winthrop D. Jordan, *White Over Black: American Attitudes Toward the Negro, 1550-1812* (Chapel Hill, 1968), pp. 167-78 (quotation, p. 169).

3. Eugene D. Genovese, *Roll, Jordan, Roll: The World the Slaves Made* (New York, 1974), pp. 327-28, 414, 429-31; (quotations, pp. 429, 431).

4. Robert William Fogel and Stanley L. Engerman, *Time on the Cross: The Economics of American Negro Slavery* (Boston, 1974), pp. 130-39.

5. Carl N. Degler, *Neither Black Nor White: Slavery and Race Relations in Brazil and the United States* (New York, 1971), (quotation, p. 102), pp. 107, 182-83, 231, 242-44.

6. Ira Berlin, *Slaves Without Masters: The Free Negro in the Antebellum South* (New York, 1974), pp. 178-79.

7. U.S. Bureau of the Census, *Population of the United States in 1860 . . .* (Washington, D.C., 1864), p. xii.

8. [Henry F. James], *Abolitionism Unveiled! Hypocrisy Unmasked! and Knavery Scourged! . . .* (New York, 1850), p. 28; *De Bow's Review*, 8 (March 1850), pp. 587-88.

9. Alexis de Tocqueville, *Democracy in America*, 2 vols. (New York, 1956), I:379.

10. Harriet Martineau, *Society in America*, 2 vols. (New York, 1837), I:384, 393; II:114-18.

11. Frederick Law Olmsted, *A Journey in the Seabord Slaves States, with Remarks on Their Economy* (New York, 1863), p. 18; Frederick Law Olmsted, *A Journey in the Back Country* (New York, 1863), p. 385. Mary Boykin

Chestnut's observations on mulattoes in the South have become a familiar historical reference. The South Carolinian wrote in her diary: "Like the patriarchs of old, our men live all in one house with their wives and their concubines; and the mulattoes one sees in every family partly resemble the white children. Any lady is ready to tell you who is the father of all the mulatto children in everybody's household but their own. Those, she seems to think, drop from the clouds." Mary Boykin Chesnut, *A Diary from Dixie*, ed. Ben Ames Williams (Boston, 1949), pp. 21-22.

12. Fogel and Engerman, *Time on the Cross*, p. 132; Tocqueville, *Democracy in America*, I:374.

13. La Roy Sunderland, *Anti-Slavery Manual, Containing a Collection of Facts and Arguments on American Slavery*, 3d ed. (New York, 1839), pp. 29-30.

14. Charles Sumner, *The Barbarism of Slavery: Speech of Hon. Charles Sumner, on the Bill for the Admission of Kansas as a Free State* . . . (Washington, D.C., 1860), p. 27; Charles Grandison Parsons, *Inside View of Slavery: A Tour Among the Planters*, 2 vols. (Savannah, Ga., 1974), I:84.

15. David Lee Child, *The Despotism of Freedom; or, The Tyranny and Cruelty of American Republican Slave-Masters* . . . (Boston, 1833), pp. 54-55; (quotation, p. 55).

16. Philo Tower, *Slavery Unmasked: Being a Truthful Narrative of a Three Years' Residence and Journeying in Eleven Southern States* . . . (Rochester, 1856) (quotations, pp. 322-23); John Lawrence, *The Slave Question*, 4th ed. (Dayton, Ohio, 1857), pp. 212-13; Horace Greeley, ed., *The Writings of Cassius Marcellus Clay: Including Speeches and Addresses* (New York, 1848), p. 181.

17. William G. Brownlow, *Ought American Slavery to be Perpetuated? A Debate Between Rev. W. G. Brownlow and Rev. A Pryne Held at Philadelphia, September, 1858* (Philadelphia, 1858), p. 222.

18. Ronald G. Walters, *The Antislavery Appeal: American Abolitionism after 1830* (Baltimore, 1976), p. 73.

19. Tower, *Slavery Unmasked*, pp. 307, 316-24; Sunderland, *Anti-Slavery Manual*, pp. 29-30; Child, *The Despotism of Freedom*, p. 55; Martineau, *Society in America*, II: 114-18. Ronald G. Walters offers an excellent discussion of this subject in *The Antislavery Appeal*, pp. 72-76.

20. [George Bourne], *Slavery Illustrated in Its Effect upon Woman and Domestic Society* . . . (Boston, 1837), pp. 48-50, (quotations, p. 62), 101.

21. Jules Zanger, "The 'Tragic Octoroon' in Pre-Civil War Fiction," *American Quarterly* 18 (Spring 1966), pp. 63-70.

22. "Governor Hammond's Letters on Slavery—No. 2, *"De Bow's Review* 7 (December 1849) p. 494.

23. John Campbell, *Negro-Mania: Being an Examination of the Falsely Assumed Equality of the Various Races of Men* . . . (Philadelphia, 1851), pp. 471–72.

24. *The Pro-Slavery Argument; As Maintained by the Most Distinguished Writers of the Southern States* . . . (Charleston, 1852), p. 44; Harper, "Slavery in the Light of Social Ethics" in *Cotton is King, and Pro-Slavery Arguments* . . . (Augusta, Ga., 1860), pp. 582–83; *see also* William Gilmore Simms's arguments in *The Pro-Slavery Argument*, pp. 228–30, and in his anonymous, *Slavery in America, Being a Brief Review of Miss Martineau on That Subject* (Richmond, 1838), p. 40.

25. [Simms], *Slavery in America*, pp. 38–40; (quotation, p. 40).

26. Cobb, *An Inquiry into the Law of Negro Slavery in the United States of America* (Philadelphia and Richmond, 1858), ccxii, ccxix–ccxx; (first and third quotations, p. ccxx; second, p. ccxix).

27. Olmsted, *A Journey in the Seaboard Slave States*, p. 108.

28. [Simms], *Slavery in America*, p. 40.

29. E. Franklin Frazier, *The Negro in the United States* (New York, 1949), p. 274; Berlin, *Slaves Without Masters*, p. 151; Parsons, *Inside View of Slavery*, I:42–43.

30. Olmsted, *A Journey in the Seaboard Slave States*, pp. 421, 426–29.

31. James H. Johnston, *Race Relations in Virginia & Miscegenation in the South, 1776–1860* (Amherst, 1970), pp. 231–36; Berlin, *Slaves Without Masters*, pp. 3, 6, 151, 180; Parsons, *Inside View of Slavery*, I:82–84.

32. [Simms], *Slavery in America*, p. 51.

33. Frederick Douglass, *Life and Times of Frederick Douglass, Written by Himself* (New York, 1941), pp. 71–72. Douglass reports that he learned afterward that the help had really come from Wilk's friends in Baltimore and Annapolis.

34. Silvia Hoffert, "This 'One Great Evil,'" *American History Illustrated* 7 (May 1977), p. 38.

35. Frazier, *The Negro in the United States*, pp. 274–76; Johnston, *Race Relations*, p. 293.

36. John Dixon Long, *Pictures of Slavery in Church and State* . . . (Auburn, 1859), pp. 22–23.

37. Tocqueville, *Democracy in America*, I:379.

38. Clement Eaton, *The Mind of the Old South* (Baton Rouge, 1967), p. 172; Berlin, *Slaves Without Masters*, pp. 57–58.

39. "Black and Mulatto Population of the South," *De Bow's Review* 8 (June 1850), p. 588; [James], *Abolitionism Unveiled*, p. 28.

40. Berlin, *Slaves Without Masters*, p. 198.

41. L. S. M., "Negro-Mania," *De Bow's Review* 7 (May 1852), pp. 519–20.

42. Olmsted, *A Journey Through Texas; or, A Saddle-Trip on the South-western Frontier* (New York, 1857), p. 57; Olmsted, *A Journey in the Seaboard Slave States*, pp. 18–19, 92; Tower, *Slavery Unmasked*, p. 325.

43. Parsons, *Inside View of Slavery*, I: (quotation, pp. 42–43), 82–84.

44. Harriet Beecher Stowe, *Uncle Tom's Cabin, or, Life Among the Lowly*, ed. Kenneth S. Lynn (Cambridge, Mass., 1962) (quotations, pp. 8, 7, 15, 271, 15, 25). Slave narratives gave similar stress to the attractiveness of near-white slaves. See, for example, William W. Brown, *The Narrative of William W. Brown, a Fugitive Slave* (Reading, Mass., 1969), pp. 11, 63; *Running a Thousand Miles for Freedom, or, The Escape of William and Ellen Craft from Slavery*, in Arna Bontemps, ed., *Great Slave Narratives* (Boston, 1969), pp. 271–72.

45. George M. Fredrickson, *The Black Image in the White Mind: The Debate on Afro-American Character and Destiny, 1817-1914* (New York, 1971), pp. 115–18.

46. Stowe, *Uncle Tom's Cabin.* p. 274.

47. Berlin, *Slaves Without Masters*, p. 196; Long, *Pictures of Slavery in Church and State*, p. 24; Johnston, *Race Relations*, p. 185. For related discussions concerning the whites' lack of trust in mulattoes and "town niggers" see George Fitzhugh, *Cannibals All!, or Slaves Without Masters*, ed., C. Vann Woodward (Cambridge, Mass., 1960), p. 200; Edward A. Pollard, *Black Diamonds Gathered in the Darkey Homes of the South* (New York, 1859), pp. 57–61.

48. Johnston, *Race Relations*, p. 298.

49. Ibid., pp. 300–301.

50. Josiah Clark Nott, "Statistics of Southern Slave Population," *De Bow's Review* 4 (November 1847), pp. 277–85; Josiah Clark Nott, "Nature and Destiny of the Negro," ibid., 10 (March 1851), pp. 330–31. Nott offered a longer discussion of these and related ideas in *Types of Mankind: or, Ethnological Researches, Based upon the Ancient Monuments, Paintings, Sculptures, and Crania of Races, and upon Their Natural, Geographical, Philological and Biblical History . . .* (Philadelphia, 1854).

51. For a discussion of the place of Nott's arguments in scientific debates of the period see Fredrickson, *The Black Image*, pp. 76–81; Thomas F. Gossett, *Race: The History of an Idea in America* (Dallas, 1963), pp. 58–61; William R. Stanton, *The Leopard's Spots: Scientific Attitudes Toward Race in America, 1815-59* (Chicago, 1969), pp. 66–76 (quotations 66, 68).

52. Nott, "Nature and Destiny of the Negro," (first two quotations, pp. 330–31); Nott, "Statistics of Southern Slave Population," (third quotation, pp. 284–85).

53. Stanton, *The Leopard's Spots*, pp. 176–79, 189–94.

54. J. H. Van Evrie, *Negroes and Negro "Slavery": The First an Inferior Race: The Second Its Natural Condition* (New York, 1861), v-vii, 17–38, 125–67 (first quotation, p. 146; second, p. 161; third, p. 167; fourth, p. 163).

55. Ibid., pp. 17–33, 144–45, 161–63. For other examples of interest in the debate over hybridity *see* James A. Stewart, *Powers of the Government of the United States* . . . (Washington, D.C., 1856), p. 15; *De Bow's Review* 10 March 1851), p. 364. Frederick Law Olmsted showed his curiosity about the issue by asking residents in the lower South about the longevity of mulatto families in the area. The residents' comments did not appear to support the sterility theory. *See* Olmsted, *Journey in the Back Country*, pp. 90–92.

56. Henry Cleveland, *Alexander H. Stephens in Public and Private* . . . (Philadelphia and other cities, 1866), pp. 721–723.

From Slavery
to Fettered Freedom:
Attitudes Toward the
Negro in Brazil*

Racial prejudice in nineteenth-century Brazil never became as severe or inflexible as in the American South, because Brazil had had long experience with miscegenation and a tradition of the mulatto escape hatch. Brazilian defenders of slavery could not develop the strict color test of superiority and inferiority that prevailed in the United States. Yet prejudice was a force in Brazilian society, and it grew in intensity during the crisis over abolition. In the Brazilian context this bigotry usually took the form of harshly negative assessments of the Negro's capacity for freedom. Brazilians usually phrased their criticisms euphemistically, complaining about the "manpower problem," but their language turned more virulently anti-Negro when they were confronted with the threat of complete emancipation.

The problems created by this veiled form of prejudice were poignantly addressed by a planter-politician from São Paulo named Paula Souza. In April 1888 Paula Souza sent a letter to several newspapers proposing a solution to the coffee planters' "manpower" problems. He wrote at a time of great apprehension, for thousands of slaves were fleeing from their masters, leaving the coffee planters without workhands to tend the crops. Paula Souza tried to assuage the planters' fears by noting that many of the fugitives were beginning to

*The author's original version of "From Slavery to Fettered Freedom: Attitudes Toward the Negro in Brazil" Luso-Brazilian Review, vol. 7 (Summer 1970) (© 1970 by the Regents of the University of Wisconson), pp. 3-12 are reprinted here in revised form by permission.

return to work. He then urged his colleagues to reconsider their attitude toward black labor in order to cushion the shock of the impending abolition of slavery. Why should so many *fazendeiros* insist on working either with slaves or European immigrants, he asked? Why not consider a third alternative—the black freedmen? "We have an enormous body of workers upon which we were not counting," he explained. "I do not allude to the immigrant who today is seeking us in abundance; I refer to the Brazilian, a sluggard yesterday. . . . This Brazilian today devotes himself to labor, either because this has become more respectable through liberty, or because his former resources have failed him. This is what we are seeking here."[1]

The appeal of Paula Souza highlights one of the central issues in the debate over the abolition of slavery—the reluctance of *fazendeiros* to exchange their labor force of Negro slaves for Negro freedmen. When abolitionism became the great issue of the 1880s, many Brazilian planters, especially those of the coffee regions of the Central-South, responded by attempting to maintain chattel slavery as long as possible or by insisting that full emancipation could not take place until sufficient numbers of European immigrants could be found to replace the slave workers. Few coffee *fazendeiros* showed much initiative in recruiting the ex-slaves, despite the fact that the ranks of the black freedmen could easily supply one of the largest and most immediately available sources of labor after abolition. This chapter is designed to explore the reasons behind the attitudes of the planters and the implications of these attitudes for the postemancipation status of blacks in Brazil.

The coffee planters' strong resistance to emancipating their bondsmen is closely related to the way they viewed the manpower issue. During the nineteenth century, the slave population in Brazil did not increase sufficiently to meet the needs of the planters. While the slaveholders could easily replenish their supply of servile laborers through human traffic from Africa, the mortality rate among slaves remained very high, significantly exceeding the birth rate. With the cessation of the Atlantic slave trade in the 1850s and the rise of coffee production in southern Brazil, new sources of labor had to be found. Some planters reacted to the problem by encouraging the propagation of slave children. But most planters from the Central-

South dealt with their manpower needs principally by purchasing slaves from the Northeast. This supply dried up, however, when laws were passed in the 1880s to halt the interprovincial traffic. With the intensification of the antislavery movement in the 1880s, the question of labor supply became even more pressing.[2]

Basically, three types of planters played the most significant roles in the debate over abolition in the 1880s, and they viewed the manpower problem from different perspectives. These major groups can be identified as the planters of (a) the Northeast, (b) the Paraíba Valley—southern Minas Gerais region, and (c) central and western São Paulo. These categories represent a simplification of the situation, as the division is not all-inclusive and, in many cases, the positions overlapped. Still, generally speaking, the classification is represent-ative of the most salient differences among planter groups.

The *senhores de engenho* of the sugar-cane regions of the Northeast had a superfluous number of slaves in the 1880s. Suffering from an extended depression of the sugar industry in Brazil, they tried to cut costs by selling some slaves and liberating others. As the freedmen in the Northeast were limited in their movement because of the small market economy, poor cities, and semidesert hinterland conditions, a large percentage of them remained as marginal men, connected to their masters' plantations through social and economic ties of paternalism and indebtedness.[3] Many Northeastern planters did not fear that the abolition of slavery would adversely affect labor recruitment; they advocated emancipation through their own initiative.[4]

Slaveholders in the Central-South were far more hostile to abolition-ism. Many of the most adamant slavocrats lived in the older coffee regions of the Paraíba Valley (which stretches through Rio de Janeiro and part of São Paulo) and in southern Minas Gerais. Most of these *fazendeiros* had an adequate supply of slaves in the 1880s, the Paraíba group having acquired them from the African slave trade and the interprovincial slave trade, while the Minas planters secured bondsmen from the depressed mineral regions of their province. Although these older coffee lands had been the center of riches in the mid-nineteenth century, the economic debility of the region was now evident—caused to a large degree by the planters' inefficient agri-cultural methods and the consequent soil exhaustion. But the *fazendeiros* of the Paraíba-Minas Gerais area did not arrange a favorable accommodation with free labor as did their Northeastern counterparts. While the demand for Brazilian sugar was declining in the world market, the demand for Brazilian coffee was rising. Despite their economic problems, these coffee *fazendeiros* did not wish to cut the size of their work force or risk disruption of their production. Believing that emancipation would upset the work routine, they refused to substitute freedmen for slaves.[5]

Fazendeiros from the dynamic, expanding coffee regions of central and, particularly, western São Paulo faced a different problem. They did not have sufficient bondsmen to meet their demands; in fact, the most important source of new slaves, the interprovincial slave traffic, was closed to them in the 1880s at the time of their great expansion into the rich new lands of western São Paulo. Consequently, the Paulista planters sought to increase the immigration of Europeans into Brazil. Despite much progress in this work in the decade of the eighties, however, they were not completely satisfied that the influx of foreigners was sufficient to allow them to support abolition. Although many of these planters believed that free labor was more efficient and productive than slave labor, they refused to advocate immediate and total emancipation.[6]

The reluctance of the planters of the Central-South to divorce themselves from slave labor was reflected in the parliamentary debates. Planters of the Paraíba-Minas Gerais group stressed that their entire economic and social system was based on slavery, while the São Paulo *fazendeiros* pleaded for sufficient time to make the transition to immigrant labor.[7]

An explanation of the *fazendeiros'* opposition to emancipation must also go beyond the manpower issue, as many other significant factors were related to the problem. After all, if the planters of the Central-South were in such great need of laborers, why could they not accept abolition and work with the freedmen? Certainly, the resistance to emancipation can partly be explained by the desire of rural leaders to maintain their tremendous social prestige and political power— benefits that they believed only a slaveholders' regime could give them. Also, many of the *fazendeiros* of the Paraíba Valley were heavily in debt, and they did not wish to incur the added expense of wage payment. But another important reason for the resistance to emancipa-

tion cannot be overlooked. Abolition would force the slave proprietors suddenly to face the backfire of years of exploiting their
captives. The coercive nature of slavery would prove a distinct
liability to the planters after emancipation. They feared that the
bondsmen, who had been forced to labor all of their lives, would
exploit the new opportunities of freedom by evading their work.[8]

Many of the slave proprietors' fearful predictions proved correct—
at least in the short run. In an environment of great abolitionist agitation in the last year before the emancipation decree, thousands of
Negro bondsmen fled from the plantations, and the structure of the
slave regime began to collapse. Such emigrations continued even after
abolition was officially declared. Excited by the chance to escape
formal discipline, the freedmen wandered in the countryside or
gathered in the congested cities. The long experience in slavery left
many of the liberated unprepared for freedom. They lacked interest
in the goals of property ownership and family security and thought
that emancipation would make leisure an attainable blessing. When
the freedmen did remain on the plantations, it was often for only a
limited period. They worked long enough to "buy" their leisure,
showing little initiative for accumulating savings beyond their
subsistence needs. Consequently, the *fazendeiros* often found the
freedmen's labor undependable and not very productive.[9]

During the years of the great debates over abolition, slaveholders
criticized the abolitionists for not considering the seriousness of
these problems. They did not care to recognize their own culpability
in the difficulties or understand that the freedmen's desire to evade
work would be, for the most part, only a temporary reaction in celebration of liberty. Nor did the slave proprietors admit that the unat-
tractive incentive system they offered their employees was much to
blame for the response of apathy. Instead, the *fazendeiros* exploited
the issue of the "unreliable freedmen" as ammunition in their bitter
verbal war against abolitionism. Slavocrat Antônio Coelho Rodrigues,
for example, explained that "there are two main problems in the
slavery question: to free the slave from captivity and to incorporate
the freedmen into civil society." He suggested that the abolitionists
had shown themselves incapable of providing a solution for the second
problem. "If they had more prudence in their plans, and more probity
in their means," asserted Coelho Rodrigues, "they would be a party

of the future, and not limit their views to simple liberation of the Negroes."[10] Other proslavery literature contained similar arguments. The slavocrats alluded to stories about freedmen who dissipated their energies and engaged in antisocial behavior—the "realities" to which they said the abolitionists were blinding themselves.[11]

The Negro slaves were not sufficiently educated to become respectful citizens, insisted the slavocrats. Slaves had not acquired the proper habits to be able to accept liberty responsibly.[12] What guarantees did the society have that the freedmen would not abandon their work and cluster in the cities as paupers, vagabonds, and criminals? To prevent this problem, the state would have to pass new laws to compel the freedmen to remain at their jobs, punish delinquents, and augment the police forces to guarantee the security of individuals and property.[13] Otherwise, the blacks would have license to run away from the plantations and create civil disorders.

In arguing that the blacks were unprepared for freedom, some of the slavocrat statements smacked of racial prejudice. Scholars have often claimed that extensive mixing of the races in Brazil made relationships there between blacks and whites smoother than in other countries, particularly the United States.[14] There is certainly much truth in this argument, but such a comparison should not lead to an underestimation of the seriousness of the bigotry that did exist in Brazil. Slavery in Brazil established patterns of human relationships that easily engendered racial prejudice. As C. R. Boxer notes, one race cannot systematically enslave another for 300 years without acquiring a feeling of racial superiority.[15] When Brazilian slaveholders sought to justify the continuance of the servile institution while confronting the abolitionist attack, their condescending attitudes toward the Negroes became manifest.

The Brazilian positivist philosopher, Luís Pereira Barreto, was direct and frank in his expression of racial prejudice. In a series of articles featured in the *Província de São Paulo* Barreto, a slaveowner, asserted it was a scientific fact that the "Aryans" were superior to the Negroes as evidenced by greater intelligence and progress in human evolution toward civilization. It was senseless to offer immediate liberty to the Negroes, he declared, because freedom would be useless in their hands and would only increase their impatience. Barreto cautioned the abolitionists against "dumping in the center of the society a horde of semibarbaric men, without direction, without a social goal, without savings, and what is more distressing yet, in an age that does not permit them to reconstruct their education." Barreto believed that liberating thousands of dangerous slaves could bring a conservative reaction that would make the Negroes' condition even worse than under slavery.[16]

Arguing in the same spirit, the editors of the proslaveholder newspaper *O Cruzeiro* charged that the abolitionists did not understand the unreliable nature of the slave. When not obligated to work, the Negro would turn to crime and vagabondage "like a savage animal of the African deserts." "The animal instinct in them is superior to reason," added the editors.[17]

A propaganda pamphlet disseminated by the Commercial Association of Rio de Janeiro also expressed apprehension about making the Negroes freedmen. The truth is, claimed the Association, "that in Brazil, as all over, the freedman is incompatible with any regime of economy, order, labor and morality." It described the free Negroes as "miserable" individuals who were ignorant of their rights and duties and without a proper notion of morality. Abolition would have to wait until some adequate plan could be arranged to provide for "the adaptation of an inferior and uneducated race to the precepts of the civilization and the social state of the other races."[18]

Abolitionists responded to these slavocrat arguments by accepting some of the facts but drawing different conclusions. They were ready to admit that the slaves were not fully prepared for freedom. Abolitionists saw this condition as the result of slavery and, therefore, another reason for extinguishing it. For example, abolitionist writer and orator J. Simões agreed that the Negroes had been kept ignorant under slavery, and the Bahian abolitionist Luís Anselmo Fonseca believed they had to be carefully protected and guided. "The slave is a little more than a brute and a little less than a child," said Fonseca.[19] But the abolitionist differed from the slavocrats in that they proposed to do something about the slaves' social and economic deficiencies. Throughout the antislavery campaign, abolitionists discussed and presented numerous projects to help the Negroes make new adjustments as freedmen.

Antislavery leaders said that their goal had to be more than just simple liberation; they needed to prepare the blacks for civic and economic life through moral and vocational instruction. They claimed that in the United States the abolitionists had done excellent work in educating the freedmen, and, consequently, the blacks there acted like civilized men, not "barbarians."[20]

The means that abolitionists suggested to help the emancipated blacks adjust to freedom varied according to the personal orientations of the particular individuals. Many of the abolitionists' suggestions were designed to keep the blacks working in agriculture. André Rebouças, a mulatto who showed great interest in agrarian reform, wished to see the government give the freedmen land. He thought that if the blacks could become individual proprietors, they would have a stake in society and become more industrious.[21] Joaquim Nabuco, leader of the abolitionist forces in Parliament, sought to link the freedmen to the land through arrangements similar to the immigration colonization programs, while J. Simões suggested guaranteeing the planters a contract for labor services after abolition as a means of keeping the blacks in agriculture.[22] A plan submitted by Senator João Manuel de Souza Dantas provided specific deterrents for those who would stray from the land; it included a rural code, a work law, and a law to prevent vagrancy.[23]

Many proposals asked that the government provide special supplies and training for the liberated slaves. The above-mentioned projects of Rebouças and Simões called for the establishment of special schools to educate the freedmen, while the Dantas plan suggested that the government establish colonies for agricultural work to educate the *ingénuos* (children of slaves born free after the Rio Branco Law of 1871) and to provide employment for the freedmen. The Liberator Society of Ceará wanted special care and training for the women and children who were freed from slavery, while a multi-faceted project presented in the newspaper *Gazeta da Tarde* asked that freedmen be guaranteed a minimum wage and be given primary school instruction as well as food, clothing, and shelter. For the planters, the project suggested a law to force the freedmen to remain in their present occupation and a law to penalize vagabondage.[24] Some educational projects were carried out by the abolitionists' own initiative. For example, João Clapp, the president of the Abolitionist Confederation, and Luiz Gama, a mulatto abolitionist leader in São Paulo, operated night classes for slaves and freedmen.[25] Thus, many abolitionists believed that the work force of Negro freedmen could help the planters to solve the manpower problem, and they proposed specific programs to strengthen the Negroes' role in that solution. Unfortunately, the abolitionist movement ended with the extinction of slavery. As Joaquim Nabuco later sadly commented, "the abolitionist current stopped the day of abolition and receded the following day." No complementary social measures were passed to benefit the liberated or to define their new social status. They were given only juridical freedom.[26]

The abolitionists were not entirely to blame for the simplicity of the emancipation law. During the last years of their campaign, when the institution of slavery was collapsing and becoming discredited, many political leaders who earlier had shown little interest in the plight of the blacks jumped on the antislavery bandwagon and called themselves "abolitionists." Hence, the "Golden Law" of May 13, 1888, was passed by legislators representing multifarious interests; it was not solely a product of the hard-core abolitionists.[27] After abolition, political power remained in the hands of the great *fazendeiros*— leaders who were often indifferent to the social and economic problems of the freedmen.

Emancipation did not result in any significant change in the position of the free Negro in the Brazilian social structure. In a society of rigid class lines, he was left on the lowest rung of the social ladder. The new, emerging order was a competitive society, and the freedman was ill-prepared to participate in it. Some women found urban jobs in domestic service, and the freedmen who had acquired special skills found positions as artisans. But, for the large majority, particularly those freed from the plantations, the opportunities were limited to temporary, insecure, and degrading jobs. A marginal men in the economy, they formed the occupational groups that worked for the lowest wages. Many who had joined the exodus to the cities established *favelas* (shanty towns), while others returned to the rural areas, becoming subsistence farmers or sharecroppers.[28]

At the time when abolition was decreed, many *fazendeiros* believed that foreign immigrants would serve their manpower needs better than the native black population. Particularly in southern Brazil (in the region from São Paulo to Rio Grande do Sul) business and agricultural leaders saw the immigration of white Europeans as a panacea for the labor problem. They thought that these foreigners, particularly Italians, were more dependable and productive workers than the ex-slaves; and also the planters feared that the presence of the black freedmen might deter the Europeans from emigrating to Brazil. As the immigrants poured into Brazil in the late 1880s, *fazendeiros* gained new confidence.[29] Ironically, at the same time, many of the freedmen sobered to the responsibilities of earning a living as the adventure of irresponsible liberty and leisure seemed to lose its attraction. The desire to celebrate the new status, which was understandable in light of the experience in bondage, gave way to a new interest in finding employment. Freedmen began returning to the *fazendas*, but for many it was too late. *Fazendeiros* turned them away, declaring that the ex-slaves' temporary absences from the plantations were examples of "Negro ingratitude" in response to their master's emancipatory actions. The *fazendeiros* declared their preference for foreign labor, believing that the freedmen were "vagabonds"—a group of "irresponsible" or even "useless" people.[30]

In the twentieth century some Negroes and, particularly, mulattoes found positions of social and economic importance in Brazilian society. Notwithstanding some subtle forms of discrimination, they never confronted institutions of racial prejudice as overt and harsh as those that troubled blacks in the United States in the same period. Yet the glaring reality remained that an extraordinarily disproportionate number of blacks in Brazil were locked into the culture of poverty, and, to a great degree, this problem could be traced to the heritage of slavery. Long after the servile institution was destroyed, its victims continued to suffer from the repercussions of the experience in bondage. Without land, deficient in education, and stigmatized in the eyes of much of the white population, the ex-slaves and their descendants found their opportunities limited. Despite the potentiality of social ascendancy for people of color, other economic and social barriers were not easy to surmount. The legacy of the slave past cast a heavy shadow, hampering the efforts of Brazilian blacks to challenge the obstacles.

Notes

1. *Rio News,* April 15, 1888, p. 3.
2. João Pandiá Calógeras, *A History of Brazil* (Chapel Hill, 1939), pp. 145–50, 189; Caio Prado Júnior, *História Econômica do Brasil* (São Paulo, 1949),

pp. 163–78; Emília Viotti da Costa, "O Escravo na Grande Lavoura," in *História Geral da Civilização Brasileira*, Sérgio Buarque de Holanda, ed. (São Paulo, 1966), 5:161; Celso Furtado, *The Economic Growth of Brazil* (Berkeley 1963), pp. 127–34.

3. Celso Furtado, *The Economic Growth of Brazil*, pp. 151–52; Charles Wagley, *An Introduction to Brazil* (New York, 1963), pp. 106–14, 165–71.

4. Tobias do Rêgo Monteiro, *Pesquisas e depoimentos para a História* (Rio de Janeiro, 1913), p. 58; Jorge Freire, *Notas à Margem da Abolição*, *Mossoró—Rio Grande do Norte* (n.p., n.d.), p. 6; Herbert H. Smith, *Brazil: The Amazons and the Coast* (New York, 1879), pp. 467–70.

5. Stanley Stein, *Vassouras: A Brazilian Coffee County, 1850–1900* (Cambridge, 1957), pp. 229–30, 242–46; Associação Commercial do Rio de Janeiro, *Elemento Servil* (Rio de Janeiro, 1884), p. 4; *O Abolicionismo perante a história ou o diálogo das trés proviníncias* (Rio de Janeiro, 1888), p. 87; *Annaes da Câmara do Parlamento Brasileiro* (1880), 4: 446; *Vinte e Cinco de Março*, May 11, 1884, p. 3; *Rio News*, October 15, 1888, p. 3.

6. Nazareth Prado, ed, *Antônio Prado no império e na república* (Rio de Janeiro, 1929), pp. 53–57; *Rio News*, October 5, 1883, p. 2; January 24, 1884; February 15, 1884.

7. *Annaes da Câmara do Parlamento Brasileiro* (1884), 1:88–89; 2:67: Prado, *Antônio Prado no império e na república*, pp. 30, 67–69, 84–87.

8. Alcindro Sodré, *O Elemento Servil, A Abolição* (Rio de Janeiro, 1942), pp. 102–103; *Annaes da Câmara do Parlamento Brasileiro* (1884), 2:50; (1885), 1:241; *Rio News*, March 24, 1884, p. 2.

9. Furtado, *The Economic Growth of Brazil*, pp. 153–54; Roberto Simonsen, "As Conseqüências econômicas da abolição," *Revisto do Arquivo Municipal de São Paulo*, 147 (May 1938): 266; *Relatório apresentado á Assembleia Legislativa Provincial de São Paulo pelo Presidente de Província Exm. Snr. Francisco de Paula Rodrigues Alves no Dia 10 de Janeiro de 1888* (São Paulo, 1888, p. 23; Nícia Vilela Luz, "A Administração Provincial de São Paulo em face do movimento abolicionista," *Revista de Administração* (December 1948), p. 94.

10. Antônio Coelho Rodrigues, *Manual do Subdito fiel ou Cartas de um lavrador a sua magestade o Imperador Sôbre a questão do elemento servil* (Rio de Janeiro, 1884), p. 92.

11. *O Abolicionismo perante a história ou o diálogo das três províncias*, pp. 20–21.

12. *Annaes da Camâra do Parlamento Brasileiro* (1884), 1:246; *Annaes do Senado do parlamento Brasileiro* (1888), 1:42.

13. *Annaes da Câmara do Parlamento Brasileiro* (1884), 2:68; (1885), 1:139; *Gazeta da Tarde*, January 24, 1884, p. 1; *O Cruzeiro*, November 6, 1880, p. 1.

14. For relevant discussions of race relations, *see* Gilberto Freyre, *The Masters and the Slaves: A Study in the Development of Brazilian Civilization* (New York, 1961); Wagley, *An Introduction to Brazil*, pp. 132–47; Marvin Harris, *Patterns of Race in the Americas* (New York, 1964), pp. 44–94.

15. C. R. Boxer, *The Golden Age of Brazil, 1695–1750* (Berkeley, 1962), pp. 17, 142, 166, 173–76; C. R. Boxer, *Race Relations in the Portuguese Colonial Empire, 1415–1825* (New York, 1963), pp. 6, 27–29, 40, 101, 112.

16. See the *Província de São Paulo*, November 20 to November 30, 1880.

17. *O Cruzeiro*, December 20, 1880, p. 3.

18. Associação Commercial do Rio de Janeiro, *Elemento Servil*, pp. 8–10.

19. Luis Anselmo da Fonseca, *A Escravidão, o Clero e o Abolicionismo* (Bahia, 1887), p. 590; *Gazeta da Tarde*, December 11, 1882, p. 2.

20. Fonseca, *A Escravidão, o Clero, e o Abolicionismo*, p. 658.

21. André Rebouças, *A Agricultura Nacional* (Rio de Janeiro, 1883), p. 126; Inácio José Veríssimo, *André Rebouças através de sua auto-biografia* (Rio de Janeiro, 1939), p. 214; André Rebouças, *Diário e notas autobiográficas*, ed. Ana Flora and Inácio Veríssimo (Rio de Janeiro, 1938), p. 315.

22. Carolina Nabuco, *The Life of Joaquim Nabuco* (Stanford, 1950), p. 55; *Gazeta da Tarde*, December 11, 1882, p. 2.

23. *Annaes do Senado do Parlamento Brasileiro*, 1887, Sessão em 3 de Junho, pp. 16–18.

24. *O Libertador*, January 1, 1881, p. 5; *Gazeta da Tarde*, October 6, 1882, p. 2.

25. *Gazeta da Tarde*, August 1, 1882, pp. 1; April 17, 1883, p. 1.

26. Joaquim Nabuco, *Minha Formação* (São Paulo, 1934), p. 212; Nilo Odalia, "A Abolição da escravatura," *Anais do Museu Paulista* 18 (São Paulo, 1964), pp. 135–36.

27. Among the eleventh-hour abolitionists were the following important leaders in Parliament: João Alfredo, Moreira de Barros, Campos Salles and José Antônio Saraiva.

28. Stein, *Vassouras*, pp. 271–74; Alfonso de Toledo Bandeira de Melo, *O Trabalho Servil no Brasil* (Rio de Janeiro, 1936), p. 83; Florestan Fernandes, *A Integração do Negro á Sociedade de Classes*, (São Paulo, 1965), pp. 3–4, 10, 31–32, 39–43.

29. Fernandes, *A Integração do Negro á Sociedade de Classes*, pp. 9–13; Fernando Henrique Cardoso, *Capitalismo e Escravidão: O Negro na Sociedade do Rio Grande do Sul* (São Paulo, 1962), pp. 269, 312.

30. Fernandes, *A Integração do Negro á Sociedade de Classes*, pp. 16–18, 32, 49, 55; Cardoso, *Capitalismo e Escravidão*, pp. 276, 316; Octávio Ianni, *As Metamorfoses do Escravo: Apogeu e crise da escravatura no Brasil Meridional* (São Paulo, 1962), pp. 264–65; *1° Centenário do Conselheiro Antônio da Silva Prado* (São Paulo, 1946), p. 169.

PART 2:
THE PROCESS
OF ABOLITION

4.

Abolition in Brazil: The Collapse of Slavery

Students of American history have long wondered if a more compromising and moderate approach to emancipation could have been worked out rather than the tense and bloody solution achieved through the Civil War. Robert Allen Christopher, the American observer mentioned earlier for his interest in Brazil, considered the relevance of a comparative model. "In Brazil, emancipation was accomplished more slowly," noted Christopher, "and the advantages inherent in peaceful and gradual liberation of slaves are readily apparent today." Christopher was especially impressed by the absence of violence. "Because of the growing popularity of voluntary emancipation and the cumulative results of emancipatory legislation," he said, "the abolition decree of 1888 was something of an anticlimax."[1]

Christopher's picture of Brazilian abolition reflects more myth than reality. It is true that Brazilians experimented with gradualist emancipation programs more extensively than did Americans, but their efforts were not successful in bringing the desired ends. In fact, plans for moderate change often backfired when put into operation. Instead of calming the political environment and insuring a moderate pace of reform, they stirred interest in more radical solutions.

The commitment to gradualism and fear of immediate abolition was a concern of many reform-minded leaders of Brazilian society. José Tomaz Nabuco, one of the Empire's most progressive politicians made a representative statement of this view in the early 1870s. When the Brazilian parliament was preparing its first major plan for emancipation, Nabuco warned of the dangers of precipitous action. "Simultaneous and immediate abolitionism is an abysm," he warned, "because of the brusk transition of two million men from the state of slavery to that of liberty!" Fast change would bring a "fatal transition" characterized by public disorder and the "anarchization of labor," he said.[2]

In the 1870s and 1880s the Empire's politicians attempted to put a variety of moderate plans to work. Yet their efforts were stymied at almost every turn by the stubborn slaveholders' regime. As late as the mid-1880s their legislation had made very little progress in whittling down Brazil's slave population. It is ironic, then, that the fast pace of events in 1886–1888 brought about exactly the conditions that Nabuco, the gradualist, wanted to avoid. Slavery fell in Brazil amid great chaos and disorder. The society's most volatile political problem came to a quick settlement when scenes of anarchy on the plantations frightened many slave proprietors into joining the ranks of the abolitionists.

Although the end came fast for Brazilian slavery, the beginning of the end took a long time to become evident to the slaveholders. It required years of slow but significant general changes in Brazilian society before the abolitionist movement could effectively challenge the masters' regime. In the middle of the nineteenth century the transformations started to take effect. Brazil's sleepy, rural-based society began to lose its provincial appearance as the Empire underwent greater exposure to the forces of Western civilization.

Economic changes helped to create favorable conditions for an abolitionist attack on the slave system. In the second half of the nineteenth century a tremendous coffee boom in the Central-South quickened the pace of life. Soaring profits from coffee exports brought Brazil's trade into favorable balance. While commerce surged, the nouveaux riches filled their pockets with milreis and hungered to purchase European goods. Capital accumulation began to awaken the sleepy Empire. Technology put Brazil in easier contact with the rest of the world. Steamship lines and railroads speeded travel, and the telegraph revolutionized communications. The first telegraph line went into operation in 1852; by 1874 a transatlantic cable brought daily information to Rio de Janeiro about the latest events in Europe. Small industries sprouted, especially textiles. A polytechnic school opened to train engineers, while military academies gave emphasis to

special technical training and exposed cadets to ideas that linked
modernization to nationalism.   *free labor more profitable*
them slavery

To many people excited by these developments—merchants and
commercial agents, lawyers and doctors, engineers, students, military
men, and even some members of the planter class—slavery seemed
incompatible with the new emerging order. They condemned slavery
as an obstacle to development and praised free labor as much more
profitable than sluggish slave labor. None of the advanced nations
rested their productive efforts on a servile work force, they said.
Free Labor was essential to the development of a modern civilization.[3]

The drive to place Brazil among the world's "civilized" nations
inspired Brazilians to copy the cultural and political trends of
modernizing societies. Brazilians carefully watched for changes in
European fashions and made exaggerated efforts to imitate the British
and the French. Men dressed in the "British cut," and women tried
to bring Parisian-style refinement and culture to Rio de Janeiro.
Similarly, Brazilians studied the literary and political moods of
Europe, a practice that left them disturbed because of the fashionable
antislavery views of the day. Their embarrassment seemed especially
acute when they traveled to Europe and came face-to-face with
criticism of their country or when British and French antislavery
societies sent well-publicized letters of complaint to the Brazilian
government. News of abolition in the United States jarred them, and
reports of progress toward emancipation in Cuba added to their
discomfort. Brazil seemed to be isolated as the last nation in the
western hemisphere still committed to slavery. "The eyes of the world
are upon us, judging us barbarians, savages . . .," exclaimed one
annoyed senator.[4]

The growing economic and philosophical pressures weakened
slavery's popular support. By the 1860s, many Brazilians believed that
something had to be done to set slavery on the road toward ultimate
extinction. Although these leaders would endorse only a gradual,
long-range program, they believed that something had to be done
to show the Empire's commitment to the ideal of emancipation.

As pressure for action intensified, arguments about turning reform
ideas into action developed into disputes between proponents of
voluntary manumission and advocates of government action.

Many individuals were sympathetic to "the emancipation idea" but opposed setting precedents for governmental intervention. Sílvio Romero, a prominent literary critic, warned against government meddling in the affairs of slaveholders and asked that emancipation be left to the voluntary actions of the proprietors.[5] Many believed that an attempt to take bondsmen away from masters would be tantamount to an attack on property. When these individuals saw pressures for emancipation mounting, they raised the cry for indemnification. By insisting that proprietors be fully compensated for all slaves freed by the government, they left their opponents with little choice but to reject a tax bill that the country could not practically accept.[6] Abolitionists were not prepared to pay masters for property they considered illegal; and plantation owners, who represented the richest potential tax base in the Empire, were hardly likely to favor paying a large part of the cost of freeing their own slaves.[7]

In addition to emphasizing the legal and financial difficulties of emancipation, opponents of governmental intervention said there was little need for state interference, because slavery could be expected to pass away naturally. To support this thesis, they claimed that the close of the African slave trade would retard the growth of Brazil's slave population. Slave mortality had always been high, they argued, and an adequate work force of servile laborers had been maintained through constant replenishment from the Atlantic trade. With this source of laborers now cut off by Brazil's 1850 law abolishing the Atlantic traffic, the number of slaves could be expected to diminish rapidly from low reproduction and the effects of voluntary manumission.[8]

In terms of demography slavery actually did decline in some regions of Brazil after the end of the African slave trade. The Northeastern coastal section of the country, once a rich sugar plantation area, suffered from economic decline. Demand for slaves from the Northeast grew in the Central-South (around the provinces of Rio de Janeiro, São Paulo, and Minas Gerais), where the coffee boom led to rapid development of new plantations. This demand for manpower stimulated an active interprovincial slave trade. The exchange rapidly depleted the population of young and healthy slaves in some Northeastern regions. Many Northeastern planters liberated the slaves they could not sell, especially the aged and infirm. The demographic changes loosened the Northeastern planters' ties to slavery, and some of them and their sons became outspoken proponents of emancipation reform.[9]

The Paraguayan War (1865–1870) did much to strain Brazilian politics and bring the slavery controversy into the open as a volatile issue that could not be evaded. The drawn-out war engaged Brazil, Argentina, and Uruguay in an alliance against the forces of Paraguay's frenzied dictator, Francisco Solano Lopez. When Brazil did not quickly achieve the expected easy victories, attention focused on the government's poor handling of mobilization efforts. As the political squabbles grew, leaders began to make recommendations for general "reform," suggestions that went well beyond the issue of military preparedness.[10] Among these ideas was a call for legislation to spur emancipation of the slaves. In 1867 the French Emancipation Committee helped give the issue an important boost by sending an open letter to Emperor Dom Pedro, asking that he intervene in behalf of the slaves. The Brazilian government replied that emancipation was simply" a question of form and opportunity and that appropriate action would be taken after the end of hostilities with Paraguay. The words of this reply became famous. With the restoration of peace in 1870, emancipation advocates saw "opportunity" at hand. Through parliamentary debates, they now pressed for a settlement on the "form" of change.

By 1871 Emperor Dom Pedro realized that the delicate subject of slavery could no longer be sidestepped. Pedro had been sympathetic to the idea of emancipation, but he worried that he could lose valuable political support if he appeared in the vanguard of reform. Many of the Empire's largest slaveholders opposed even moderate changes. To cushion himself against the inevitable political shock waves, Pedro tried two strategies. First, he turned to a leader of the Conservative party to head the ministry that would prepare a new emancipation proposal. By appointing the Viscount of Rio Branco as new chief minister, Pedro hoped to placate intransigent slavocrats who opposed any emancipation legislation associated with the Liberal party.

Second, Dom Pedro disassociated himself from Parliament's decision by leaving on an extended trip to Europe before the heated parliamentary discussions began. In his absence Princess Isabel became the titular spokesman for the throne.

After months of emotional debate, Parliament settled on a compromise solution that became known as the Rio Branco Law (also

*law of
Free
Birth*

frequently called the Law of Free Birth).[11] The new legislation provided freedom for slaves belonging to the Imperial government, protection of the slave's right to maintain private savings (the *pecúlio*) for purposes of purchasing his freedom, registration of all slaves in the Empire, and establishment of an emancipation fund from the proceeds of taxes and government lotteries. Most important, it announced that after passage of the law all children born of slave mothers would be legally free. Such children became known as *ingenuos*. But the "free birth" measure contained an important qualification. In order to satisfy indignant slaveholders who wanted to delay the law's impact and establish the principle of compensation, the law watered down the significance of the ingenuos' freedom. Until ingenuos reached the age of twenty-one, masters would have the right to retain them for services. If the masters did not wish to hold ingenuos for the entire period, they could turn them over to the state at age eight and receive 600 milreis (about $300) as compensation.

Complications notwithstanding, the Rio Branco Law seemed a great national achievement. When Parliament finally voted it into law in September 1871, the Brazilian people joined in a huge celebration. As the United States minister watched jubilant citizens in the galleries toss flowers down on members of Parliament, he picked up some of the colorful plants and said, "I am going to send these flowers to my country in order to show how a law was made here, in this manner, which cost so much blood there."[12] Similarly, many Brazilian reformers hailed the law as an example of sensible compromise. The Rio Branco Law helped to avert a violent confrontation over slavery, and it set up the machinery for gradual abolition, they said. Now all the sources of slavery had been cut off. Abolition of the Atlantic slave trade represented the first milestone in this effort; with the Rio Branco law no additional people would be introduced into the slave population. By concentrating henceforth on cutting away at the existing population of bondsmen, complete abolition could be accomplished in a generation. The combination of voluntary manumission, compensated emancipation, freedom by self-purchase, and slave mortality would tear at the institution from different angles, gradually leading to orderly extinction.

For the next eight years, slavery remained largely outside the political spotlight. Many former critics of slavery were content to give the government time to test the machinery of the Rio Branco Law. Indeed, the very existence of complex legislation seemed to ease the consciences of many citizens. At least the nation had taken a bold step, they thought; and by doing so, it had made a crucial commitment to freedom. Slaveholders also found reason to remain calm. They came to realize that the legislation was much less injurious to them than they had first believed. The law did not emancipate many slaves, yet it gave the appearance of reform. Whenever opponents raised questions about slavery, the proprietors stressed the need to work within the framework of the Rio Branco Law—legislation that, they insisted, provided the proper channels for dealing with slavery.[13]

After eight years of relative quiescence, in 1879 the emancipation issue broke into the open again, especially in the Chamber of Deputies. With the return of the Liberal party to control of the chief ministry, several young, talented, and reform-minded deputies made their debuts. They quickly found reason for a fight. In the opening discussions slavocrats made the mistake of broaching the slavery issue themselves. They spoke nervously about recent reports of slave uprisings and called for extending the deterrent powers of government to discourage violent insurrections.[14] Then Jeronymo Sodré, a Liberal and a professor of medicine from Bahia, responded with a ringing speech against slavery that reopened the old wounds of 1871.[15] In the weeks to follow other abolitionist politicians joined the battle in Parliament, most notably Joaquim Nabuco, a young, handsome, dynamic deputy form the northeastern province of Pernambuco and son of Senator José Tomas Nabuco. The younger Nabuco quickly became the most outstanding abolitionist orator in Parliament as well as a prolific journalist and a leader in abolitionist organizations.

In 1880 abolitionism spread beyond the halls of Parliament, becoming an active movement in major cities of the Empire. New abolitionist newspapers and pamphlets appeared in the streets, making the slavery question again an issue for popular public discussion. Numerous clubs formed to coordinate local campaigns. Modeling their organizations on the example of earlier antislavery activities in England and the United States, these groups planned lobbying strategy, promoted public meetings, collected funds for propaganda publications, and sometimes attempted to purchase freedom for selected slaves. The clubs became especially strong in the capital city

abolition programs

of Rio de Janeiro. By sponsoring elaborate programs in local theaters that drew many people from the upper echelons of Brazilian society, these organizations helped give the burgeoning movement respectability.

Afro-Brazilians became much more openly involved in this new phase of antislavery activity. In the early 1880s several Afro-Brazilian figures began to draw national attention.

In the city of São Paulo, Luiz Gama achieved prominence as a lawyer who successfully defended the slaves' efforts to win freedom in the courts. Gama's father was a Bahian planter of distinguished Portuguese background; his mother was a street vendor who claimed ties to African tribal royalty. Gama spent his early years in relative comfort on his father's plantation; but bad economic fortunes put the estate deeply into debt, and the father sold his ten-year-old son into slavery. After being shipped south to São Paulo, Gama befriended educated tenants in the home where he worked and developed his skills in reading and writing. Eventually, he escaped from his master and obtained proof of free birth. Through many years of labor as a journalist, lawyer, organization leader, and political activist, Gama established an impressive record working for the slaves' cause. He died in 1882, just as the antislavery movement in Brazil's fastest-growing province started to gain momentum.[16]

Another leading Afro-Brazilian in the movement, André Rebouças, tried to use his friendship with the Imperial family to further the cause of freedom. Rebouças, a mulatto, was the son of a distinguished lawyer and politician. He achieved a notable career in engineering at a young age by planning the construction of some of Brazil's first railroads. Emperor Dom Pedro and his daughter Isabel were impressed by the breadth of Rebouças' intellectual interests and his capacity for philosophic reflection. Their respect and fondness brought Rebouças special invitations to the Imperial estate. Though many mulattoes with Rebouças' education and acceptance in high social circles tended to tread lightly on the sensitive issue of slavery, Rebouças refused to divorce himself from the plight of the less fortunate. Although shy by nature, he spoke openly and emotionally about his black "brothers" in bondage and identified himself proudly as an abolitionist partisan. Rebouças particularly emphasized land reform, hoping that abolition would lead to the distribution of property to the freedmen.[17]

José do Patrocínio, the most famous of the Afro-Brazilian abolitionists, achieved fame as one of the "radicals" of the campaign. His father was a clergyman, *fazendeiro*, and politician; his mother was a free Negro grocery huckster. Although Patrocínio's father did not legally recognize his son, he gave Patrocínio favored treatment and helped subsidize his education in pharmacy school. Patrocínio had great difficulty finding gainful employment in his new profession but soon discovered profits and popularity in a different endeavor: journalism. He began writing columns for a leading Rio de Janeiro periodical, then obtained capital to purchase his own newspaper, the *Gazeta da Tarde*. Patrocínio turned the *Gazeta* into the most important abolitionist organ in the Empire. By offering fiery journalistic style and tough literary lashings against the slavocrats, his editorship sent the newspaper's sales spiraling. Not content to unleash his anger only in the newspaper office, Patrocínio carried his campaign to the city streets. His public appearances as a dynamic orator upset many Imperial politicians. They worried that Patrocínio's street appearances before large crowds of Afro-Brazilians could stir trouble. Even moderate abolitionists warned that his harangues might provoke violence, jeopardizing their efforts to negotiate a solution in Parliament.[18]

Although moderate and radical abolitionists disagreed strongly about programs and strategy during the early 1880s, they were usually able to bring their forces together for the purpose of writing manifestos or drafting legislation. One of their most important early legislative efforts developed out of a project Joaquim Nabuco submitted to the Chamber of Deputies in 1880, calling for complete emancipation of the slaves by January 1, 1890. *Fazendeiros* put up fierce resistance and easily defeated it in the Chamber by an overwhelming vote of 77-16.

Between 1881 and 1884 abolitionists pushed for piecemeal legislation in attempts to eat away at the legal props for slavery. Some invoked an Anglo-Brazilian treaty of 1831 that declared that all slaves imported from Africa thereafter should be set free. Abolitionists knew tens of thousands of Africans had been brought to Brazil illegally after the signing of the treaty. If the 1831 agreement could be implemented in the courts, many slaves would have to be released, including the offspring of illegally imported Africans.[19] This judicial approach to abolition produced few successes, however. Not until the last two years of slavery did lawyers begin to attain some significant court victories based on the 1831 treaty. *Stopping slave traffic* The campaign to halt the interprovincial slave traffic was more successful. Significantly, this reform effort won substantial support from the slaveholders themselves. *Fazendeiros* from the Central-South began to worry about a growing political disequilibrium created by the large-scale demographic shift in the slave population. A continued drain on the slave population of Northeastern Brazil would probably lead politicians from that region to vote more sympathetically for abolitionist legislation.[20] Moreover, coffee *fazendeiros* were apprehensive about the increasing incidence of slave insurrection involving bondsmen recently imported from the Northeast. One political leader from São Paulo warned his colleagues, "You *fazendeiros* who buy slaves from outside are placing assassins in your homes, not laborers."[21] The coffee planters who had already purchased an adequate supply of slave labor and worried about these dangers helped provide the votes necessary to close the domestic slave trade in several major provinces.

Although these reform drives attracted moderate enthusiasm, the strongest pressures for reform related to new, broad measures to remedy the defects of the Rio Branco Law. The Law of Free Birth, which looked like progressive legislation in 1871, now seemed a plum for the slavocrats. Instead of truly accelerating emancipation, the Rio Branco Law in practice freed only a small percentage of Brazil's slaves. Discovering the supposed lion to be only a mouse, slaveholders rallied to defend the law in the 1880s, praising it as a definitive program for abolition and insisting that no major changes were necessary. In fact, by asserting their support for the Rio Branco Law, slaveholders noted proudly that they were not retrograde slavocrats like Southerners in the antebellum United States. Capitalizing on the presence of a law that committed the nation ultimately to abolition, they boasted of their endorsement of long-range emancipation. "In Brazil we are all emancipators," said one proslavery spokesman; "there are no more slavocrats."[22]

Abolitionists now viewed support for the Rio Branco Law as little more than a commitment to see slavery abolished sometime in the twentieth century. Conceivably, a bondsman born of a slave mother one day before September 28, 1871, might still be enslaved as late as 1950, at the age of 79. Statistics confirmed the pessimism of the abolitionists. According to one widely circulated report, the total slave population declined by 329,873 from 1874 to 1883, but only 18,900 of this decline represented slaves released through the emancipation fund. A much larger proportion of the decline could be attributed to deaths (195,348) and voluntary manumissions (115,625).[23] Most slaves were left to "emancipation by death," as one abolitionist described the situation. Furthermore, years of experience showed that the ingenuos—children born "free" of slave mothers but remaining in tutelage until age twenty-one—were being treated as slaves. Masters subjected them to the regimen of the regular slave forces. In fact, planters often worked the ingenuos especially hard in order to exploit maximum production before releasing them. Thus, the "free birth" idea, one of the most celebrated aspects of the Rio Branco Law, began to look like a cruel hoax.[24]

With abolitionist pressure growing, Emperor Dom Pedro recognized the need for a political change in 1884. He turned to the Liberal senator Manoel Pinto de Souza Dantas to form a new ministry and prepare legislation to compensate for the weaknesses of the existing emancipation laws. Dantas' son presented the ministry's program in Parliament. The project's most notable innovation was a promise of immediate freedom for all slaves over sixty years of age. It also called for an increase in the emancipation fund through new taxes, termination of the interprovincial slave trade throughout the Empire, and immediate liberation of slaves not properly registered. Finally, the legislation proposed a table for the progressive amortization of slave values over a period of years, a schedule that presumably would allow freedom for a slave when his officially established value reached zero.

Just as in the case of the Rio Branco project, proslavery leaders mounted a powereful assault to weaken provisions of the Dantas plan. They persisted in their policy of obstruction with such determination that, after a long and frustrating effort, the Dantas ministry fell in 1885. Dom Pedro then handed the reins of government to another

Liberal, José Antônio Saraiva, whose political record was more acceptable to the slaveholders. Following more months of tense debate, most of Saraiva's modifications won approval and a new law began to take shape. But Dom Pedro worried about the political repercussions of the reform law and tried to guard against them. He turned to the Baron of Cotegipe, a Conservative party leader and noted defender of slaveholding interests, to preside over official passage of the new legislation. As in the case of the Rio Branco Law, the Emperor allowed a Conservative to put his stamp on a major emancipation bill in an attempt to please the landed aristocracy.[25]

The new legislation, which passed on September 28, 1885 (the fourteenth anniversary of the Rio Branco Law), became known as the Saraiva-Cotegipe Law. In its final form the bill took much of the bite out of the original Dantas proposals. It recognized the slaveholders' concern for the principle of "indemnification" by applying qualifications to emancipation of the elderly. Slaves age sixty-five and over would be totally free, but those between the ages of sixty and sixty-five were obligated to a term of labor services to their masters. In many cases the term would extend for three years. The beefed-up emancipation fund still fell far short of the need. Although the Saraiva-Cotegipe Law planned for complete emancipation within thirteen years, the monies provided could help to free only a small percentage of the slave population in that period. The final bill also dodged the issue of freeing slaves not properly registered by adopting hazy language about requirements for registration. Moreover the revised plan modified Dantas' original proposals concerning gradual liberation based on amortized values and age. The Saraiva-Cotegipe Law substituted different tables that, in effect, prolonged the period of waiting for emancipation. Finally, to calm the slaveholders' growing fear of slave escapes, the law established a heavy fine for enticing or sheltering fugitives.[26]

Emasculation of the original Dantas project stirred many frustrated abolitionists into becoming radicals and immediatists on the emancipation issue. Years of careful efforts to produce gradual abolition now seemed abortive. Compromise and patience had brought little progress, they thought. Before the Dantas controversy, most leading abolitionists cautioned against precipitous action and urged their followers to work within the legal system. After humiliating setbacks and passage of the Saraiva-Cotegipe Law, abolitionists began speaking much more stridently about strategy and tactics. They demanded immediate and unconditional emancipation—a liberation decree unfettered by special provisions, qualifications, and subtle loopholes that could later be interpreted to the benefit of slaveholder-controlled governments. Moreover, many abolitionists shouted a new war chant, calling on supporters to abandon their pledge to keep campaign activities within the confines of the law. "No one is obligated to respect slavery," fumed José do Patrocínio. "On the contrary, every citizen ought to combat it by every means. Against slavery all means are legitimate and good."[27] Abolitionists now broadened the scope of their activities. Rather than limiting propaganda to persuading the free population, they began appealing directly to the slaves. Some recommended flight; others even countenanced rebellion.

In 1887 much upheaval took place in the plantation areas of the Central-South, as abolitionists turned to radical tactics and restive slaves took advantage of the growing turmoil. In the abolitionists' most daring acts, agents slipped into slave quarters at night to convey information about possibilities for escape and describe plans by urban citizens to hide fugitives in their homes. Antônio Bento, an intensely religious antislavery leader in the city of São Paulo, developed elaborate machinery for an "underground railroad." Working through a church brotherhood made up mostly of slaves and freedmen, he coordinated a series of bold escape plots. Bento's exploits brought a wave of upheaval in São Paulo province in late 1887 and early 1888.[28] Several São Paulo cities fell into the control of abolitionists and became havens for fugitives. As slaves became aware of the new acts of defiance, opportunities to find refuge, and the slaveholders' weakening police power, thousands fled from the plantations to seek asylum in urban centers. The city streets then turned into battlegrounds as police and local hirelings of the slaveholders attempted to search for runaways. Slaves and freedmen openly defied the invaders. Sometimes they exchanged gunfire with police forces and slavecatchers. They also joined other urban citizens to form mobs who taunted officials at the jailhouses and railroad stations, distracting them sufficiently to help captured fugitives flee before they could be returned to the plantations.[29]

The tumultuous situation brought tragic confrontations along the roads of São Paulo province. In one violent episode a freedman and associate of Antônio Bento named Pio led his enslaved family and about 150 fugitives in an effort to reach asylum in the port city of Santos. Fiercely determined to reach his destination, Pio beat off several attempts by police forces to halt the march of runaway slaves. About forty of his followers carried arms; with cries of "Liberty or Death!" they exchanged gunfire and frightened away the troops. As the news of Pio's defiant group swept through the surrounding countryside, nervous *fazendeiros* gathered a force of thugs to plan an ambush and abruptly end the challenge that regular law enforcement officials seemed unable to check. The formation of a slaveholders' vigilante group worried the policemen. Because they wished to prevent a slaughter, they attempted to warn Pio of the impending attack. Exhausted, without food for several days, and skeptical of police intentions, Pio angrily struck down the officer who presented the warning and ordered his followers to continue marching. Other policemen reacted immediately by killing Pio. Then they retreated to allow the fugitives to go on their way. Within a short time, the band of runaways became victims of an ambush. Many were killed or captured; a few escaped and eventually made their way to Santos.[30]

In the city of Santos, which became a Promised Land to fugitives in late 1887, an Afro-Brazilian named Quintino Lacerda achieved notable success. Lacerda, a former slave, stirred up slave rebellions, aided escapes, and organized resistance forces to intervene against troops sent to apprehend fugitives. In Santos he managed the construction of a mud-and-straw, African-style fortress-city—a *quilombo* (community of runaway slaves) called Jabaquara. Lacerda set up an administration to govern the city. He also stimulated commercial activity and obtained a subscription to finance some of the building. With Lacerda's deft handling the fame of Jabaquara spread quickly.[31]

Early in 1888 the upheaval and chaos spread to other plantation areas of Brazil's Central-South. In Rio de Janeiro province, bondsmen fled to the city of Campos and to the Imperial capital of Rio de Janeiro. Fugitives in Minas Gerais gathered in the provincial capital of Ouro Preto. *Fazendeiros* saw little hope of arresting the flights once escape efforts became massive and urban centers fell into the control of abolitionists. Moreover, any effort to counter such wide-

military on slave's side

spread disorders required the cooperation of the military. In late 1887 the military made its position clear: the army would not intervene in behalf of the slaveholders. Several factors influenced this important decision. First, the military had been engaged in disputes with the Cotegipe ministry related to personal animosities, affairs of "honor," appropriations for the armed forces, and differences over the proper role of the military in government. The angry military officers were hardly enthusiastic about rescuing the Cotegipe ministry in its hour of crisis. Second, the military had little to gain by intervening with force to defend an institution that seemed to be in its last stages of life. The army would surely incur public wrath for assuming the role of slavecatcher. Finally, many military officers as well as regular soldiers had long been unsympathetic toward slavery. Coming from urban backgrounds rather than from the plantation classes, some even participated in abolitionist clubs. In the crucial period of upheaval the military chose not to act, a decision tantamount to supporting the abolitionists.[32]

By early 1888 the institution of slavery was greatly weakened from the breakdown of its coercive powers. Not only did *fazendeiros* lack the police power to challenge flights and rebellions; they also lacked the legal power to take strong punitive measures against insubordinate slaves. Antislavery gains in the courts and in Parliament succeeded in hampering the proprietors' efforts to control their human property. In the cities, magistrates became increasingly sympathetic to the slaves' cause and granted liberty on legal technicalities in some well-publicized cases. In the past it had been extremely difficult for slave litigants to win emancipation in court, even when the grievances were well founded, because slaveholders could influence the judges' decisions.[33] Now even the provincial authorities reacted to changing public sentiment and began hearing testimony from slaves who complained about poor treatment. Perhaps most important, antislavery forces in Parliament succeeded in passing a law in 1886 prohibiting use of the whip to punish slaves. The lash, long considered the masters' and overseers' symbol of power, no longer could be used as an impressive threat against troublesome bondsmen. Slaveholders considered the decision a mortal blow to their authority on the plantations and a measure that undoubtedly would lead to greater insubordination. One senator assessed the consequences in blunt terms, arguing, "Slavery cannot be maintained without corporal punishment."[34]

In March, April, and May of 1888 events moved quickly toward the dissolution of slavery. In an environment of upheaval and violence many proprietors of large plantations tried to prevent further flights by granting unconditional liberation to all their slaves. Several important leaders in Parliament who had been loud defenders of slavery now turned around 180° and called for immediate abolition. Municipalities from diverse sections of the Empire announced complete emancipation within their borders.

Isabel faced the crisis while her father was away in Europe. With political agitation mounting, she tried to encourage the Baron of Cotegipe to step down.[35] Cotegipe, last hope of the slavocrats, was in no position to resist effectively. He was overcome with difficulties. An incident of violence between police and navy personnel in the capital city intensified public outcries against his ministry, but the police/navy clash was only the surface of Cotegipe's iceberg of troubles. Already many prominent planters viewed his handling of the slavery controversy much too reactionary for the circumstances. Finally Cotegipe stepped aside, and Isabel turned to a more flexible conservative politician, João Alfredo.

By the time Parliament gathered in Rio de Janeiro in May 1888, it was clear that even minor refinements and delays in an abolition law would not be acceptable. Most of the important coffee *fazendeiros* of the Central-South now demanded an end to civil strife. Spokesmen for the Northeastern planters had little difficulty responding to the turnabouts of their southern colleagues. Many of the sugar planters had already progressed well along the way toward exchanging slave labor for free labor. Moreover, they became apprehensive about some new incidents of slave flights in their own region, developments that suggested that sections of the Northeast, too, might soon face dislocations similar to those plaguing the Central-South. After hearing a few last desperate speeches by diehard slavocrats, Parliament settled for a very simple decree that read:

> *Article 1*: From the date of this law slavery is declared abolished in Brazil.
>
> *Article 2*: All contrary laws are revoked.

Although the disorder and violence developing out of the activities of the abolitionists and slaves helped put into motion the final collapse of slavery in Brazil, it cannot be said that this pressure produced significant and lasting improvement in the condition of the liberated. Many of the Empire's leaders reached for the abolitionist banner primarily because they feared greater disorders if the government refused to grant emancipation. They did not act out of deep concern for the fate of the Afro-Brazilians. Some political abolitionists remained in Parliament after passage of the "Golden Law," but their numbers were small, and they lacked the political clout necessary to pass further legislation to assist the freed blacks. Seasoned abolitionist campaigners such as Joaquim Nabuco tried to convince national leaders that the freedmen needed help beyond the emancipation decree, but they made little headway.[36]

Unlike the scene in the United States, where some significant but awkward efforts were made to give the freedmen economic, educational, and political aid in the decade after emancipation, Brazilian politicians turned to other matters. Soon after passage of the abolition law, government leaders became preoccupied with the question of indemnification for the slave proprietors. Angry landlords demanded compensation for the bondsmen they had lost; and while they tied up the political debates with disputes about their own economic woes, there was little discussion of the problems of many black Brazilians who had already given their masters a lifetime of labor without compensation. So great was the pressure for indemnification that a few years later Rui Barbosa ordered the government's slave registration records destroyed so that the details of former slave ownership could not easily be traced.

The record of slavery's extraordinarily fast demise in Brazil raises questions about the government's experiments with a variety of programs for gradual emancipation. How effective were the attempts to bring moderate reform? Did the legislation help to move the society away from its attachment to slavery without the "fatal transition" that had worried Senator José Tomaz Nabuco?

The programs did make a great impact on the movement towards change, but not quite in the manner imagined by the original proponents of gradual reform. Each new piece of legislation, each new government commitment to the ideal of freedom, excited the hopes of the bondsmen and emboldened them to risk their personal safety if opportunities for flight—and fight, if necessary—appeared near. The blacks' reactions showed the wisdom behind the Brazilian slaveholders' nervous warning that attempts to tinker with slavery would only hasten its end. They knew that, in the most fundamental sense, slavery was a coercive institution that depended on the absolute authority of the master for its security. Effective control required that the slave view the master's power as unchallengeable and his own condition as unchangeable. But once the slave became aware of society's serious debates concerning the injustice of his status, his awe for the institutional controls faded quickly, and he became a very troublesome form of property.

Notes

1. For general studies of the abolition of slavery in Brazil, see Robert Brent Toplin, *The Abolition of Slavery in Brazil* (New York, 1972); Robert Conrad, *The Destruction of Brazilian Slavery, 1850-1888* (Berkeley, 1972); Emília Viotti da Costa, *Da senzala á colônia* (São Paulo, 1966); Robert Slenes, "The Demography and Economics of Brazilian Slavery: 1850-1888" (Ph.D. diss., Stanford University, 1975).

2. Undated letter from Charles Sumner to José Tomaz Nabuco in the Joaquim Nabuco Collection of the Instituto Joaquim Nabuco, Recife, Brazil.

3. Richard Graham, "Causes for the Abolition of Negro Slavery in Brazil: An Interpretive Essay," *Hispanic American Historical Review* (May 1966), pp. 123-37; Roberto C. Simonsen, *A evolução industrial no Brasil* (São Paulo, 1939), pp. 24-25; Stanley J. Stein, *The Brazilian Cotton Manufacture: Textile Enterprise in an Underdeveloped Area, 1850-1950* (Cambridge, 1957), pp. 7-9, 18; José Maria dos Santos, *Os republicanos paulistas e a abolição* (São Paulo, 1942), p. 170; Richard Graham, *Britain and the Onset of Modernization in Brazil* (Cambridge, England, 1968), pp. 31-32; Octavio Ianni, *Raças e classes sociais no Brasil* (Rio de Janeiro, 1966), pp. 78-93.

4. Ypiranga, *Breves considerações histórico-polítcas sôbre a discussão do elemento servil na Camara dos Deputados* (Rio de Janeiro, 1871), p. 17; Augusto de Carvalho, *O Brasil: Colonisação e emigração* (Porto, 1876), p. 94; *Annaes do Senado* (1871), September 26, p. 251.

5. Luiz Luna, *O negro na luta contra a escravidão* (Rio de Janeiro, 1968), pp. 180-83; Evaristo de Moraes, *A campanha abolicionista: 1879-1888* (Rio de Janeiro, 1924), p. 32.

6. *Annaes da Camara* (1884), 1:245; Luis Anselmo Fonesca, *A Escravidão, o clero e o abolicionismo* (Bahia, 1887), p. 295; *Associação Commercial do Rio de Janeiro: Elemento Servil* (Rio de Janeiro, 1884), p. 5.

7. Joaquim Nabuco, *A Campanha abolicionista no Recife* (Rio de Janeiro, 1885), pp. 36–37.

8. Joaquim Caetano da Silva Guimaraes, *A agricultura em Minas* (Rio de Janeiro, 1865), pp. 9–10; Agostinho Marques Perdigão Malheiro, *A escravidão no Brasil,*, 2 vols. (Rio de Janeiro, 1866-1867), 2:157-58; Lacerda Werneck, *Ideias de colonização,* pp. 21–24.

9. Peter Eisenberg, "Abolishing Slavery: The Process on Pernambuco's Sugar Plantations," *Hispanic American Historical Review* (November 1972), pp. 580–97.

10. Graham, *Britain and the Onset of Modernization in Brazil,* p. 23; Malheiro, *A Escravidão no Brasil,* 2:118; Orlando de Almeida Prado, *Em defenza da raça: O preconceito de raça não existe no Brasil* (São Paulo, n.d.), pp. 3–4, Edison Carneiro, ed., *Antologia do negro brasileiro* (Rio de Janeiro, n.d.), pp. 46–48.

11. Evaristo de Moraes, *A lei do ventre livre* (Rio de Janeiro, 1917).

12. Tobias do Rego Monteiro, *Pesquisas e depoimentos para a história* (Rio de Janeiro, 1913), p. 34.

13. Robert Brent Toplin, *The Abolition of Slavery in Brazil,* p. 131.

14. *Annaes da Camara* (1879), March 3 and March 5; Joaquim Nabuco, *Discursos parlamentares: 1879–1889* (São Paulo, 1949), pp. 6, 10–11.

15. *Annaes da Camara* (1879), March 5, pp. 194–96.

16. Sud Mennucci, *O precursor do abolicionismo no Brasil: Luiz Gama* (Rio de Janeiro, 1938); Moraes, *A campanha abolicionista,* pp. 250–58; Richard Morse, *From Community to Metropolis: A Biography of São Paulo, Brazil* (Gainesville, 1958), p. 146; Dorothy B. Porter, "The Negro in the Brazilian Abolition Movement," *Journal of Negro History* (1952), pp. 61–62.

17. André Rebouças, *Diário e notas autobiográficas,* eds. Ana Flora and Inácio José Veríssimo (Rio de Janeiro, 1938); Inácio José Veríssimo, *André Rebouças Através de sua autobiografia* (Rio de Janeiro, 1939); Porter, "The Negro in the Brazilian Abolition Movement," pp. 66–70; Moraes, *A campanha abolicionista,* pp. 34–37.

18. Moraes, *A campanha abolicionista,* pp. 355–76; Osvaldo Orico, *Patrocínio* (Rio de Janeiro, 1935); João Guimaraes, *Patrocínio: O abolicionista* (São Paulo, 1956); Ciro Viera da Cunha, *No tempo de Patrocínio* (São Paulo, 1960); Porter, "The Negro in the Brazilian Abolition Movement," pp. 61-62; *Gazeta da Tarde,* May 29, 1884, p. 1; Carneiro, *Antologia do negro brasileiro,* pp. 398–404.

19. *O Abolicionista,* January 1, 1881, p. 3; *O Paiz,* October 9, 1887, p. 1;

Manifesto da Confederação Abolicionista do Rio de Janeiro (Rio de Janeiro, 1883), pp. 8–9; Joaquim Nabuco, *O abolicionismo* (São Paulo, 1938), p. 221.
20. *Rio News,* May 24, 1882, pp. 4–5; *Annaes da Assemblea Legislativa Provincial de São Paulo* (1881), June 18, pp. 469–70.

21. *Annaes da Assemblea Legislativa Provincial de* São Paulo (1878), March 27, pp. 474, 478–79.

22. Antonio Coelho Rodrigues, *Manual do subdito fiel ou cartas de um lavrador a sua magestade o Imperador sôbre a questão do elemento servil* (Rio de Janeiro, 1884), p. 6; *Rio News,* July 5, 1884, p. 3; *O Cruzeiro,* December 20, 1880, p. 3; Fernando Henrique Cardoso, *Capitalismo e Escravidão* (São Paulo, 1962), p. 239; *Rio News,* October 15, 1880, pp. 3–4; Luiz Monteiro Caminhoa, *Canna de assucar e café—relatório apresentado ao governo* (Rio de Janeiro, 1880), p. 104; Baron of Cotegipe to J. Arthur de Sousa Correa, March 9, 1888, Instituto Joaquim Nabuco; *Diário do Brazil,* May 10, 1884, p. 1.

23. Monteiro, *Pesquisas e depoimentos para a história,* pp. 71–72.

24. Ruy Barbosa, "Emancipação dos escravos, in *Obras completas de Ruy Barbosa* (Rio de Janeiro, 1945), 40:8. Also, *see* Joaquim Nabuco, *Abolitionism: The Brazilian Antislavery struggle,* ed. Robert Conrad (Urbana, 1977).

25. *O Paiz,* October 18, 1887, p. 1; Herbert H. Smith, *Brazil: The Amazons and the Coast* (New York, 1879), pp. 516–17.

26. Osorio Duque-Estrada, *A abolição: 1831–1888* (Rio de Janeiro, 1918), pp. 165–68.

27. *Gazeta da Tarde,* June 22, 1886, p. 1.

28. *Revista do Instituto Histórico e Geográfico de São Paulo* (1914), 19:635–36; *São Paulo e a sua evolução: Conferências realisadas no Centro Paulista em 1926* (Rio de Janeiro, 1927), pp. 33-35; *A Redempção, May 13, 1899,* pp. 3–4; Antonio Manuel Bueno de Andrada, "Depoimento de uma testemunha," *Revista do Instituto Histórico e Geográfico de São Paulo* 36 (1939), p. 221; José Maria dos Santos, *Os republicanos paulistas e a abolição* (São Paulo, 1942), pp. 169, 310–15; *A Redempção,* January 27, 1877, pp. 1–2; May 13, 1899, pp. 3–4; *Cidade do Rio,* April 30, 1888, p. 1.

29. Robert Brent Toplin, "Upheaval, Violence, and The Abolition of Slavery in Brazil: The Case of São Paulo," *Hispanic American Historical Review* (November 1969), pp. 639–55.

30. *O Paiz,* October 20, 21, and 22, 1887; *Diário de Santos,* October 21, 1887, p. 1; October 25, 1887, p. 1; *Correio Paulistano,* October 21, 1887, p. 1; Andrada, "Depoimento de uma testamunha," p. 224; *Relatório,* Chief of Police of São Paulo province, Salvador Antônio Muniz Barreto de Aragão, 1887, p. 6; *A Redempção,* October 27, 1887, p. 2; *Gazeta do Povo,* October 21, 1887, p. 1.

31. "Quilombolas e Jabaquara," in *O Estado de São Paulo*, June 24, 1956.

32. Duque-Estrada, *A abolição 1831–1888*, pp. 205–09, 225–26; Nelson Werneck Sodré, *História militar do Brasil* (Rio de Janeiro, 1965), p. 158; Charles Willis Simmons, *Marshal Deodoro and the Fall of Dom Pedro II* (Durham, 1966), pp. 77–94; José Maria dos Santos, *Os republicanos e a abolição* (São Paulo, 1942); C. B. Ottoni, *Autobiographia de C. B. Ottoni* (Rio de Janeiro, 1908), p. 346; *Rio News*, August 15, 1887, p. 2; *Annaes da Camara* (1888), June 4, p. 18; June 7, p. 81.

33. *Província de São Paulo*, July 19, 1887, p. 1; *Rio News*, June 24, 1887, p. 4; Rui Barbosa, *Abolicionismo* (Rio de Janeiro, 1955), pp. 37–42; *Gazeta do Povo*, November 4, 1887, p. 2.

34. *Annaes do Senado* (1886), September 29, p. 288.

35. Notes and letters of Princess Isabel, March 1888; December 1888 (?), CXCIX–9030; João Ferreira de Moura to Visconde de Paranagua, November 21, 1887; 21.11887, Arquivo do Museu Imperial; Baron of Cotegipe to J. Arthur de Sousa Correa, March 9, 1888, Instituto Joaquim Nabuco.

36. Fernando Henrique Cardoso, *Capitalismo e escravidão: O negro na sociedade do Rio Grande do Sul* (São Paulo, 1962), p. 269; Abdias do Nascimento et al., *O negro brasileiro (80 anos de abolição)* (Rio de Janeiro, 1968), pp. 3–8; Nilo Odalia, "A abolição da escravatura," *Anais do Museu Paulista* (1964) 18:138; Richard Graham, "Landowners and the Overthrow of the Empire," *Luso-Brazilian Review* (December 1970).

5.

The Specter of Crisis: Slaveholder Reactions to Abolitionism in the United States and Brazil*

The record of the Brazilian slaveholders' nervous reactions to abolitionism suggest parallels with United States history. Slaveholders in the American South voiced related fears about the abolitionist challenge, and they predicted a scenario of trouble that, in many ways, resembles the breakdown of slavery in Brazil's southern provinces. These similarities lead us to ask: To what extent did the abolitionist movements in the United States and Brazil represent real threats to the slaveholders, threats not only in the form of pressure applied toward long-term emancipation but also as immediate dangers? An understanding of the Brazilian experience should shed light on the perspective of those American slaveholders who saw secession as an answer to their problems.

In many respects the reasons slaveholders gave for their opposition to emancipation in the United States and Brazil reflected similar patterns of argument. Some of the most important concerns are immediately obvious. Simple pecuniary interest in the security of property would be one. Men who had invested heavily in servile labor would not want to see this investment suddenly decreed worthless. The threat to a whole life-style would be another primary concern of slaveholders facing an abolitionist challenge. Slaveholding

*An earlier version of "The Specter of Crisis: Slaveholder Reactions to Abolitionism in the United States and Brazil" by the author appeared in *Civil War History*, vol. 18, no. 2 (June 1972), pp. 129-38, and is reprinted here in revised form by permission.

generated a social and political world that would be altered radically if the fundamental institution on which it rested were destroyed. A fear of race adjustment in the postemancipation society also troubled the slaveholders. This problem is well documented regarding American history, but we should also be cognizant of the virulent forms of racism that pervaded Brazilian slaveholding society. The language of anti-abolitionist propaganda in Brazil in the 1880s became so laden with hostile stereotypes that the country's most famous black abolitionist, José do Patrocínio, thought, "prejudice against colored people can prolong slavery indefinitely." In both countries racism served as an obstacle to emancipation.[1] Less obvious are the potential dangers slaveholders saw in the *process* of abolition. They genuinely feared the mischief abolitionism could cause if it successfully encroached upon the ostensibly stable order of slavery. The substance of this fear deserves analysis in greater detail, first in terms of the developments in Brazil that forced a settlement of the abolition issue in 1888, and second in view of the fearful predictions made by southern secessionists in the United States.

Brazilian slaveholders actually *experienced* many of the nightmares that troubled American slave proprietors. For decades before the 1880s, Brazilian planters warned that antislavery agitation could eventually reach the slave quarters, exciting bondsmen with the idea of escape and, possibly, igniting the powder keg of servile revolt. Whether by fleeing or fighting, slaves would surely respond to abolitionist propaganda should they come in contact with it. From the perspective of slaveholders it was essential to bar the bondsmen from communication with the activities of the antislavery movement. Slaves were relatively manageable when resigned to a lifetime in bondage, but once stirred by hopes of freedom, their attitude could become rebellious.[2]

It is significant that a series of reforms that liberalized the conditions of the bondsman in the last years before abolition in Brazil did much to weaken slavery's institutional props and raise the captives' hopes for freedom. Between 1885 and 1888 various senators, government ministers, and local political and judicial reformers succeeded in winning legal guarantees for better treatment of the slaves. New laws prohibited proprietors from flogging their bondsmen; public authorities began to receive the complaints of slaves and act on their grievances; and judges, living in urban centers where abolitionism had made significant gains, increasingly delivered decisions in favor of freeing litigant captives. In a variety of cases involving the legal status of slaves, the burden of proof suddenly fell on the masters. These changes challenged what *senhores* called their "moral authority"—their ability to determine their own rules. Despite the presence of various laws to protect bondsmen and help emancipate them, proprietors had traditionally operated with minimal imposition from outside authorities. Ordinarily the *senhor* was final arbiter on his estate, a condition essential to his dominion over servile workers. The system was based on *evasion* of formal laws, not their execution. Effective control depended on the power of masters to interpret regulations according to their own interests and to exclude themselves from rules they found undesirable. Senator Silveira Martins identified the problem with sharp insight when he said, "The servile regime is an exception. When the exceptional laws disappear, slavery is finished." Developments in the 1880s showed that slavery could not be liberalized effectively and remain viable. The institution rested on coercion; liberalization undermined its foundations.[3]

Once radical abolitionists won popularity and freedom of movement in major Brazilian cities, they were able to exploit the deterioration of slaveholder control. Pockets of abolitionist agitation appeared proximate to the principal plantation areas. Major cities became asylums for runaway slaves. Unlike the American slavocrats, the Brazilian slaveholders could not contain abolitionist activities geographically. Despite serious repressive efforts, they were not able to crush discontented elements or localize them effectively. The hour was too late; neither cajolery nor coercion could check the growing urban antislavery movement inspired by both intellectual and economic concerns.

Slaveholders found troublemakers in their own backyards. Abolitionists, including many Negro freedmen, worked their way into the slave quarters at night, urged captives to flee, then slipped back into their places of refuge before daybreak. Bondsmen lost their fear of punishment as they became aware of the legal restraints on their masters' power and the new opportunities for escape. How could slavery be maintained under such conditions, asked a leading slaveholder? By the ignorance or resignation of the slaves? Hardly. In 1887 and early 1888 thousands of bondsmen made rapid exit. Many fought their way to freedom, producing firearms, slaying overseers and masters, and engaging in bloody combat when police troops tried to pursue them. By early 1888 Brazilian slavery seemed to be collapsing in a wave of upheaval, violence, and chaos.[4] Unless political leaders checked the breakdown by announcing the complete abolition of slavery, it appeared the situation would continue to deteriorate into more dangerous forms of anarchy and social revolution. Understandably, the leaders chose an emancipation decree, announcing the famous Golden Law on May 13, 1888. Making political hay of a necessary act, they hailed it as "the work of humanity, of foresight and of progress."[5]

The substantial danger of slave violence in antebellum America has not been accorded the serious treatment that it deserves. As in Brazil, the reality of the problem is often underrated in historical interpretations. Descriptions of slavery in the United States often minimize the danger of revolt by emphasizing that references to it in antebellum sources really reflect supersensitivity and emotionalism concerning slavery, racist attitudes, or a failure of the slaveowner to realize that the shoring up of slavery's institutional controls after the Nat Turner rebellion secured the proprietors against further threats of serious collective uprisings. Even in some of the finest works of scholarship, historians show reluctance to deal with the danger at face value. After offering considerable evidence for the excitement abolitionism could stir within the slave population, scholars often identify the slaveholders' protestations as examples of hysteria, irrational perception, or race anxieties.[6]

An assessment of the slaveholders' anxieties and the substance of their fears raises several questions. Was a latent readiness to revolt really a condition of the slave population? Could abolitionist literature be judged truly incendiary, as many southerners considered it? Could an abolitionist movement have eventually developed within the South itself? From the perspective of the slaveholder, were censorship and repression rational responses to a real threat? These questions lead to other queries concerning the movement toward secession. Did the Republican victory in 1860 represent a real and imminent threat to slavery? Did the slaveholders actually have much to gain by secession, assuming that independence could be achieved easily?

The fear of servile revolt persisted, as manifested in Southern speechmaking and writing throughout the antebellum period. To be sure, slaveholders did not enjoy discussing the topic, as they believed that open debate on such a volatile matter might reach the ears of the bondsmen.[7] Also, they feared that abolitionists would view affirmation of a real threat as tantamount to admitting that the South controlled freedom-loving blacks through force and coercion. When the Missouri debates brought congressmen into one of the early, frightening confrontations on the slavery issue, Edward Colston of Virginia expressed his fear that slaves might be listening to the exchanges in the galleries, and Georgia's Thomas W. Cobb warned that the antislavery challenge could kindle a fire "which seas of blood can only extinguish."[8] Indeed, James Tallmadge, Jr., the outspoken anti-extensionist whose amendment prompted the famous debates, admitted that conditions which allowed easy social intercourse between free blacks and slaves could open the way to servile war.[9]

In Thomas R. Dew's famous tract of 1832, which signaled a significant hardening of proslavery attitudes, the theme of potential insurrection flows throughout. Dew used large italics in his book for the first time on page 78—specifically for the word "insurrections."[10] In the years to follow, many leading defenders of slavery would recite the major points of his interpretation. As Dew put it, slavery was well under control as long as outside agitators did not disturb it. The blacks were usually content in their condition and loyal to their masters. In more than two centuries of slavery in the United States, there had been only a few significant attempts at insurrection. If slavery's critics should meddle in master-slave relationships, poisoning the bondsmen's minds with heinous thoughts, the tranquil African could be transformed into a "midnight murderer." Antislavery agitation was loaded with hidden deviltry. Even seemingly moderate appeals could be dangerous. Imprudent philanthropists did not understand that experimenting with the idea of emancipation could spread unrest among the slave population. The murders and destruction that attended revolts in Haiti and Virginia should not be forgotten.[11]

It is not surprising that Alfred Iverson of Georgia referred to similar dangers when he addressed the Senate in 1861 to explain his farewell

to the Union and his state's intention of joining the secession movement. Iverson predicted that Lincoln's presidency would open the
mails to incendiary abolitionist literature and establish an environment conducive to more raids like John Brown's—conditions that
would induce poisonings, murders, and revolts on an unprecedented
scale. In Iverson's view, the necessary step was clear. "We believe,"
he said, "that the only security for the institution to which we attach
so much importance is secession and a southern confederacy."[12]

Just as in Brazil then, the fear that abolitionist agitation could spark
a potentially explosive slave population was *fundamental* to the
arguments of Southern slaveholders. Racist attitudes figured in the
thinking of both groups of slaveholders, but the practical problem of
preventing a dangerous polarization of relationships between slaves
and masters also represented a primary concern. Moreover, it is
clear in the Brazilian case that the concern of slave proprietors was not
based on unrealistic, emotional fears. In the 1880s their slaveholding
order began to collapse in the face of new gains by the antislavery
forces. Whether the fears of American slaveholders were as well
founded remains to be considered. It is a question that cannot be
answered precisely because the events of the Civil War precluded a
settlement of the emancipation issue by other means. Nevertheless,
those other possibilities ought to be explored. Certainly the proprietors were cognizant of the diverse contingencies before them.

The shocking news of John Brown's raid on Harper's Ferry helped
to crystallize secessionist thought. Southerners reacted severely not
only to the John Brown raid but also to the way many Northerners
praised it.[13] Even William Lloyd Garrison, the pacifist, the non-
resistant, sounded disturbingly receptive to Brown's violent acts.
While maintaining his allegiance to pacifist principles and insisting
that Brown's rifles and spears were meant only for the slaves' self-
defense, he asserted that Brown was justified in trying to strike a blow
for freedom. Garrison gave his blessing for "Success to every slave
insurrection at the South, and in every slave country," and said,
"Rather than see men wear their chains in cowardly and servile spirit,
I would, as an advocate of peace, much rather see them breaking the
head of the tyrant with their chains."[19] Actually, Garrison's accommodation to radical, daring, attacks on slavery was mild compared
to the sanction for militant, even violent action given by many other

leading abolitionists in the late 1850s.[15] An environment propitious for slave escape and rebellion seemed fast developing.

The scenario of a troubled future that greatly worried Southerners resembled the crisis Brazilian masters feared and eventually experienced in the last years of slavery. A few of the major parallels can be mentioned. For example, Southern slaveholders felt increasingly isolated in a world growing ever more hostile to their civilization; Brazilian slavocrats lost many of their closest allies under the pressure of new currents of thought that branded slavery as anachronistic and hailed the concept of a free labor system. Southern slaveholders worried that even passage of moderate proposals to promote emancipation could open a Pandora's box of troubles; Brazilian slaveocrats discovered that gradual, reformist measures to facilitate manumission only excited the expectations of abolitionists, forcing the proprietors to try desperately to prevent reform from snowballing. Southerners worried that related issues developing out of the slavery controversy such as the concern for civil liberties and the fugitive slave law, could stimulate anti-Southern feeling among people who had been largely apathetic on the question of abolition; Brazilian slaveholders saw their efforts to silence antislavery speakers and recapture fugitives backfire to the point of making the defense of slavery seem outrageous to many of the free population, an attitude that stirred them into active support of the abolitionists. In addition to these parallels, there are others that directly concern threats to the internal stability of the slaveholding society. Southerners feared that the urban centers could become hubs for abolitionist activities and asylums for fugitive slaves, that merchants and travelers would act as emissaries of the abolitionists, and that black freedmen would join forces with their brothers in bondage in the event of a crisis. All of these problems were prominent features of the breakdown of the slaveholding order in Brazil in the 1880s.

In the American South by 1860–1861 the sound of secessionist argumentation had a comforting and logical ring to the ears of weary slaveholders who were well aware of the trends of history. They came to recognize the foresight of John C. Calhoun, whose strident voice of defiance they could not accept fully in earlier years. Were not Calhoun's prophecies borne out when the newly elected president, considered only a *moderate* Republican, had plainly stated that sooner or later slavery had to be put on the course toward ultimate extinction?[16] Once the slavery extension issue was resolved, would not Republicans turn their eyes toward that task?[17] Even the passage of very modest laws to promote emancipation might dangerously excite the slaves' expectation of freedom. And what did the Republicans have in mind as a blueprint for further political success? If the Republican leaders had any political acumen, they would certainly try to stretch their influence southward to break away from the sectional party image. Was not this thought behind the decision of sixty-eight Republican congressmen to endorse Hinton Rowan Helper's incendiary book? Had not Helper boldly tried to drive a wedge between the slaveholding and nonslaveholding whites of the South? As Helper explained, "a freesoiler is only a tadpole in an advanced state of transformation; an abolitionist is a full and perfectly developed frog."[18]

How could Republicans begin to challenge slavery internally? To many Southern secessionists the trick could be accomplished easily —without radical abolitionist legislation and without violent appeals for revolution. Republicans could eat away at slavery subtly without drawing great attention through blatant acts. They could make government patronage jobs available to abolitionists, insure that abolitionist literature could be mailed to Southern communities, appoint antislavery leaders to the federal courts, and pass new forms of taxation that would be applied specifically to property in chattel labor.[19] Even as a minority party, the Republicans could greatly capitalize on their growing popularity and their control of the governmental machinery. The Southerners who made their influence felt in national politics during the 1850s must have been keenly aware of the way a minority could wield disproportionate power in the government.

The secessionists came close to pulling off what the Brazilian slavocrats had much less chance of achieving, that is, establishment of an independent slaveholding nation that could be free of abolitionist threats for its immediate future. It is not surprising that prominent Brazilian defenders of slavery often described themselves as "the John C. Calhoun of Brazil" and hoped to resist new challenges more successfully than the South had been able to do.[20] The Brazilians could not check the growing threat, however, because they were unable to isolate the opposition geographically and, perhaps most important, the hour in history was too late for effective resistance against the antislavery forces. On the other hand, for the American secessionists of 1860–1861, independence seemed feasible, especially if it could be achieved peaceably. One after another, the southern senators made dramatic appeals in their farewell addresses, asking that their states be allowed to depart from the Union without bloodshed.[21]

Thus, a review of the Brazilian experience suggests that there may have been considerable substance behind the fears of American slaveholders. To be sure, we are dealing with a futuristic concern when discussing the Southern leaders' fears, and the fact that many of these predictions turned into reality in Brazil does not *necessarily* indicate that the same kinds of problems eventually would have developed in the United States. Moreover, the fear of internal agitation from abolitionists and slaves was not the only motivation for secession. But let us not conclude by retreating from where this analysis has been leading. If we may believe that Southern secessionists meant what they said and, indeed, that Republican ideologues meant what *they* said, then the case for secession looks strong.[22] From the point of view of the slaveholder who worried about his future security, it made good sense to try to establish peaceful secession. However, from the point of view of the present-day historian who applies moral criteria to his analysis, the case for secession obviously does not look strong. The moral side of the issue is most certainly a legitimate consideration, but it can be applied more effectively once the uncomfortable ironies of the story are recognized.

Notes

1. *Gazeta da Tarde*, Sept. 18, 1885, p. 1; *Vinte e Cinco de Março*, no. 1, May 1884. Robert Brent Toplin, "From Slavery to Fettered Freedom: Attitudes Toward the Negro in Brazil," *Luso-Brazilian Review* (Summer 1970), pp. 3–12; Robert Brent Toplin, *The Abolition of Slavery in Brazil* (New York, 1972), chs. 5 and 6.

2. For examples of this fear, see Congresso Agricola: Colleção de documentos (Rio de Janerio, 1878), pp. 47, 248–49; Rio News (Oct. 15, 1880), pp. 3–4; Feb. 5, 1882, p. 3; Gazeta do Povo, Jan. 12, 1888, p. 1; Malvino da Silva Reis, Situação ecônomica do Brasil: Exposição apresentada à comisão especial nomeda pela assembléa geral da Associação Commercial em 2 de maio de 1884 (Rio de Janeiro, 1884), p. 21.

3. Annaes da Câmara (1886), Sept. 29, p. 288; Sept. 30, p. 289; Oct. 11, pp. 307–08; Oct. 13, p. 482; Annaes do senado (1886), Sept. 29, p. 288; Província de São Paulo, July 19, 1887, p. 1; Rio News, June 24, 1887, p. 4; Gazeta do Povo, Nov. 4, 1887, p. 2.

4. Annaes da Câmara (1888), June 7, p. 93. Robert Brent Toplin, "Upheaval, Violence, and the Abolition of Slavery in Brazil: The Case of São Paulo" Hispanic American Historical Review (Nov. 1969), 639–55; Richard Graham, "Causes for the Abolition of Negro Slavery in Brazil: An Interpretive Essay," ibid. (May 1966), pp. 123–37.

5. Relatório of the Minister of Agriculture, Commerce and Public Works, Rodrigo Augusto da Silva, 1889, p. 5.

6. See, for example, David M. Potter, "John Brown and the Paradox of Leadership Among American Negroes," The South and the Sectional Conflict (Baton Rouge, 1968, pp. 203–17; C. Vann Woodward, "John Brown's Private War," The Burden of Southern History, rev. ed. (Baton Rouge, 1968), pp. 61–68; Roy F. Nichols, The Disruption of American Democracy (New York, 1948), pp. 513–17; Allan Nevins, Ordeal of the Union, 8 vols. (New York, 1947), 1:282, 507. Two outstanding recent studies that focus on South Carolina also reveal some surprisingly ambivalent statements about the problem of violence, observations that contradict the thrust of the books' evidence. See William W. Freehling, Prelude to Civil War: The Nullification Controversy in South Carolina, 1816–1836 (New York, 1968), pp. 49, 64, 358; and Stephen A. Channing, Crisis of Fear: Secession in South Carolina (New York, 1970), pp. 22–55, 78, 266–68, 289. It should be noted that Professor Freehling has refined and clarified his position on the issue. See "Paranoia and American History," The New York Review of Books, Sept. 23, 1971, p. 36.

7. Annals of Congress, House of Representatives, 16 Cong., 1 sess. (1820), pp. 1023–24.

8. Horace Greeley, A History of the Struggle for Slavery Extension or Restriction in the United States from the Declaration of Independence to the Present Day (New York, 1856), p. 9. Reports on the Denmark Vesey slave conspiracy of 1822 indicated that some of the plotters had become inspired to revolt against slavery through reading excerpts from the congressional

debates on the Missouri Compromise. Robert S. Starobin, ed., *Denmark Vesey: The Slave Conspiracy of 1822* (Englewood Cliffs, 1970), pp. 71, 84, 90, 100.

9. Greeley, *A History of Struggle for Slavery Extension*, pp. 9–12.

10. Thomas R. Dew, *Review of the Debate of the Virginia Legislature of 1831 and 1832* (Richmond, 1832), p. 78.

11. Ibid., pp. 5, 8, 63, 110, 114–25. Also, *see* William Drayton, *The South Vindicated from the Treason and Fanaticism of the Northern Abolitionists* (Philadelphia, 1836), pp. 254–75, 280–81, 299; Thomas R. R. Cobb, *An Inquiry into the Law of Negro Slavery in the United States of America* (Philadelphia, 1858), pp. clxxv, clxxvi, ccvix, ccxi–ccxii; Chancellor Harper in *The Pro-Slavery Argument* (Philadelphia, 1853), pp. 74–76.

12. *Congressional Globe*, 36 Cong., 2 sess., Senate (1860), p. 11.

13. Thomas Ricaud Martin, *The Great Parliamentary Battle and Farewell Addresses of the Southern Senators on the Eve of the Civil War* (New York, 1905), pp. 113, 156, 173; Allan Nevins, *The Emergence of Lincoln: Prologue to Civil War, 1859–1861* (New York, 1950), pp. 20, 127; Avery Craven, *Edmund Ruffin: Southerner: A Study in Secession* (Baton Rouge, 1966), p. 171. David Brion Davis points out that many Southerners viewed John Brown's raid as the fulfillment of an old prophecy, namely, that despite the abolitionists' claims of nonviolence, they really intended to stir slaves into rebellion. *See The Slave Power Conspiracy and the Paranoid Style* (Baton Rouge, 1969), pp. 34–35.

14. George M. Fredrickson, ed., *William Lloyd Garrison* (Englewood Cliffs, 1968), pp. 59–62.

15. *See*, for example: George M. Fredrickson, *The Inner Civil War: Northern Intellectuals and the Crisis of the Union* (New York, 1965), pp. 36–44; Carleton Mabee, *Black Freedom: The Non-Violent Abolitionists from 1830 Through the Civil War* (New York, 1970), pp. 318–32; Peter Brock, *Radical Pacifists in Antebellum America* (Princeton, 1968), pp. 221–39.

16. Robert W. Johannsen, ed., *The Lincoln-Douglas Debates* (New York, 1965), pp. 14, 16, 55.

17. Martin, *The Great Parliamentary Battle*, pp. 116–17, 155–68; *Congressional Globe*, 36 Cong., 2 sess., Senate (1860), p. 187; (1861), pp. 267, 271; David Christy, "Cotton is King, Or Slavery in the Light of Political Economy," *Cotton is King and Pro-Slavery Arguments* (Augusta, 1860), p. 218; Margaret L. Coit, ed., *John C. Calhoun* (Englewood Cliffs, 1970), pp. 46–47; James Williams, *Letters on Slavery from the Old World* (published by the Confederacy-Middle District of Tennessee, 1861), reprinted 1969, Miami, Florida, p. viii.

18. *Congressional Globe*, 36 Cong., 2 sess., Senate (1860), 4; Channing,

Crisis of Fear, pp. 255–56; Hinton Rowan Helper, *The Impending Crisis of the South: How to Meet It* (New York, 1860), pp. 25–27, 113, 116.

19. Eric Foner, *Free Soil, Free Labor, Free Men: The Ideology of the Republican Party Before the Civil War* (New York, 1970). pp. 5, 118–23, 134, 207–13, 313–16; Greeley, *A History of the Struggle for Slavery Extension*, p. 5; Helper, *The Impending Crisis*, pp. 156, 178; *Congressional Globe*, 36 Cong., 2 sess., Senate (1860), pp. 3–4, 11, 202–03; Hans L. Trefousse, *The Radical Republicans: Lincoln's Vanguard for Radical Justice* (New York, 1969), p. 104.

20. Martinho Campos and Andrade Figueira were especially outspoken among the proslavery leaders who identified themselves with the ideals of John C. Calhoun. *Annaes da Camara* (1880), 4:445–46; 5:72.

21. Congressional Globe, 36 Cong., 2 sess., Senate (1860), pp. 4, 11–13, 29, 33–34, 73, 189, 217; Martin, *The Great Parliamentary Battle*, pp. 179, 218.

22. Foner, *Free Soil, Free Labor, Free Men*, pp. 301–15, J. G. de Roulhac Hamilton, "Lincoln's Election an Immediate Menace to Slavery in the States?" *American Historical Review* (July 1932), pp. 700–11.

PART 3:
RACE AND CLASS IN THE TWENTIETH CENTURY

6.

Reinterpreting Comparative Race Relations: The United States and Brazil*

"With respect to race relations, the Brazilian situation is probably the nearest approach to paradise to be found anywhere in the world," said sociologist Gilberto Freyre.[1] Although this blunt statement by Brazil's noted scholar represents one of his less guarded observations, it does accurately reflect an assessment that has been popular through much of the twentieth century.[2] Students of race relations in the United States have long been fascinated with the Brazilian case, viewing it as a model of "racial democracy" that North Americans might imitate. It is little wonder, then, that when the charge of "myth" emerged from recent studies of "racial democracy" by respected scholars, the intriguing, striking contrast between the United States and Brazil suddenly appeared blurred and confused.[3] Moreover, the growth of the civil rights movement and black consciousness in the United States and the rise of new views accompanying these developments seemed to compound the difficulty of interpretation. Now what lessons could be drawn from the comparative perspective?

Many of the new comparative interpretations place modern-day race relations in the United States in a more favorable light. Some even turn the old argument around 180° to argue that the emerging pattern of racial attitudes and behavior in the United States should

*An earlier version of "Reinterpreting Comparative Race Relations: The United States and Brazil" by the author appeared in *Journal of Black Studies*, vol. 2, no. 2 (December 1971), pp. 135-55 and is reprinted here in revised form by permission of the publisher, Sage Publications, Inc.

serve as a model for Brazilians. Because it is helpful to distinguish between the older and the newer approaches to comparative race relations, I will use the terms "traditional" and "revisionist" in the ensuing discussion of interpretations. This terminology is arbitrary, of course. Divisions are not always so clear-cut, either chronologically or categorically. Nevertheless, the traditional-revisionist juxtaposition provides a useful framework for discussing the main trends in comparative viewpoints, for discerning the most salient features of interpretation. As I shall suggest, neither traditional nor revisionist views can put the intriguing questions about comparative race relations completely to rest because, to a certain extent, both approaches offer valid points. When viewed together, they especially show that the problems of race prejudice and class prejudice are related and that both deserve serious attention in a study of comparative race relations.

The once-fashionable "traditional interpretation" of race relations in Brazil, which is now being refined, stresses the importance of class distinctions over color distinctions. According to this argument class, not race, determines an individual's social status. An Afro-Brazilian who acquires a good education, achieves financial success, dresses well, and handles himself with aplomb can find acceptance in the highest social circles. He may register in Brazil's finest hotels and dine in the most exquisite restaurants. No discriminatory laws bar his entrance, and there are no separate rooms reserved especially for "colored people." Unlike the situation in the United States, achievement of class respectability can elevate a Brazilian Negro out of the stratum of the socially ostracized.[4] This acceptance of blacks who have propelled themselves upward in the class structure contrasts markedly with the "closed" system that has long endured in the United States,[5] where discriminatory legislation and community practices excluded Negroes from many establishments, forcing the black population to create separate institutions through schools, colleges, churches, and neighborhoods. No degree of individual success could guarantee a Negro's right to cross the color line. Even with the dismantlement of legal segregation since the Supreme Court decisions of the 1950s and 1960s, prejudiced attitudes remain deeply imbedded in the minds of many whites. For these groups, concern about color continues to override class considerations. Malcolm X gave a terse, graphic example of the problem: "Do you know what white racists call black Ph.D.'s? Nigger!"[6]

If the contrast between a class-conscious society and a race-conscious society puts race relations in the United States in an unfavorable light, study of specific attitudes toward race and race mixture in Brazil can make the comparison appear downright invidious. Brazil has a multicategory system for identifying race, a taxonomy that includes *cabra, pardo, moreno, mulato escuro, mulato claro,* and many other terms to classify people of color. These terms convey a general impression about physiognomic characteristics and degrees of lightness or darkness in pigmentation. Frequently, use of the Portuguese word *negro* is reserved for reference to very darkskinned individuals who seem, at least by physical appearance, to be entirely of African ancestry.[7]

According to the traditional view, this multicategory approach reflects both the heterogeneous racial composition of the Brazilian population and the liberal attitudes Brazilians display toward interracial relationships and sexual unions.[8] Historically, miscegenation occurred on such a wide scale that the famous Mexican writer José de Vasconcelos speculated that Brazil might be the first country in the Americas to achieve his ideal of forming the "Cosmic Race"— a people who were neither European, African, or Indian, but a universal mestizo type representing an amalgam of all races.[9] Again, the contrast with the United States seems dramatic. A biracial system prevails in identifying members of the "white" and "black" population in the United States. In popular terminology the individual who is not 100 percent white, even someone with very European features who is known to have a distant African ancestor, is classified as a member of the "black" community. The category of Negro takes on blanket form in the United States, covering all people with some identified African ancestry, including fairskinned mulattoes who could "pass" as whites in Brazilian society.[10] When clubs, restaurants, and hotels in the United States excluded Negroes in the era of Jim Crow, they did not make exceptions for browns or light browns. Racial "passing" in the United States only involves acceptance of individuals whom the white community *believes* to be totally of white ancestry, unadulterated by any African genetic heritage. This social reality came across forcefully in the rather melodramatic motion picture *Imitation of Life*.[11]

Thus, writers associated in varying ways with the traditional interpretation of comparative race relations have given particular attention to two factors that highlight Brazilian conditions as more fluid and tolerant than those in the United States: (1) white Brazilians emphasize class over race distinctions in accepting individuals into the social hierarchy, while white Americans often exclude coloreds on the basis of race and without regard to class position; (2) Brazil has a multiracial identification system that recognizes great variations within the population, while the United States has a biracial system that lumps all colored people in the category of "Negroes" and exposes this group to simplistic modes of classification and discrimination.

A basic shortcoming in this two-part thesis on comparative race relations derives from the significant correlation between race and class in the Brazilian social order. While whites dominate the upper stratum of society and mulattoes are prominent in the middle ranks, the truly darkskinned *negros* are concentrated in the lowest positions. In contrast to the pattern of other racial groups, a clearly disproportionate number of black Brazilians find themselves in the culture of poverty. They noticeably cluster in the economic ranks of marginal people such as day laborers, cleaning women, landless tenant farmers—in general, the inhabitants of rural shacks and urban *favelas* (shantytowns).[12]

Writers of the traditional school acknowledged this condition but largely attributed it to class. When the Negroes stepped out of slavery, explained the traditionalists, they had to compete for jobs with the limited skills learned while in bondage. Lacking property, capital, and education, freedmen and succeeding generations of blacks had difficulty establishing an economic foothold and elevating themselves on the social ladder. Yes, this group was frequently a target of prejudice, admitted the traditionalists, but it was primarily class prejudice. If an Afro-Brazilian could somehow climb the ladder of success, he could shed the stigma of the wretched class and find a place on the social hierarchy.[13]

On the other hand, "revisionists" asked of the concentration of

Brazil's blackest groups in the lowest-status positions was not related to color prejudice as well as to class prejudice. Revisionists agreed that the experience in slavery left freedmen and their ancestors with an unfortunate handicap, but they asked also whether a strong residue of race prejudice was not but another legacy of slavery. The research of a new generation of scholars, both Brazilian and foreign, uncovered considerable evidence to show that racial prejudice against Negroes was a significant feature of Brazilian society before the abolition of slavery. Contemporaries of colonial and nineteenth-century Brazil left abundant testimony of thoughts that smacked of race prejudice in their discussions about the supposedly "barbarian" civilization of Africa, the "primitive" mentality of black bondsmen in Brazil, and "scientific" ideas concerning racial distinctions.[14] The evidence also shows that these forms of prejudice lingered on after the abolition of slavery.[15] In fact, some scholars maintain that racial bigotry intensified in the postemancipation period because of reaction to the Negro's entrance into the competitive order and the influence of "scientific racism" then popular in Europe and the United States.[16]

While many traditionalists view the popular Brazilian saying "money whitens the skin" approvingly, pointing to it as evidence of the opportunity for class mobility regardless of color, revisionists regard the adage with discomfort. It implies a value judgment about color distinctions—specifically, that white is the most desirable or prestigious category and that those who, in physical terms, are not completely white may try to approximate that classification through financial success. In short, the society gives greatest reception to "white" pigmentation and physical features. Through various means, nonwhites can aspire toward identification with the ideal, the "aesthetic" physical qualities valued by society that sociologist H. Hoetink calls the "somatic norm image."[17] In Brazil successful Negroes and mulattoes can raise their rank in the order of color identification, but their desire to do so suggests that color is itself an important variable in social relations.

The position of the mulatto in Brazil illustrates the impact of the society's "whitening" ideology. While the mulatto cannot boast of unqualified credentials as a white citizen, he is aware of a range of possibilities that permit him to "pass" to a degree into the higher classes as a "conditional" white. In a syndrome quite common in

Brazil, the mulatto acts accordingly, preferring sexual unions or marriage with lighter partners, emphasizing adherence to the social values of white upper classes, shying away from reference to his Negro ancestry, and casting scorn, indeed, racial aspersions, on the Negro masses. He directs his behavior toward satisfaction of the white ideal and often cuts himself off from identification with the black population. For the very darkskinned group, recognition of this social reality can be terribly damaging to self-respect. Many dark Brazilians place hope in "purging one's blood." Women sleep with whites in order to have lighter-skinned children, and families encourage their children to complete a "good marriage" by finding a lighter mate.[18]

Color distinctions are important even within the mulatto group. By and large, opportunities for social ascendancy and acceptance are greater for the lightskinned than for the darker mulattos. A subtle sliding scale of prejudice operates to distinguish between the numerous subcategories in the mulatto group and give preference to those whose appearance best approximates the "somatic norm image."[19] To sum up, from the examples of mulattoes trying to act like whites and the evidence of white preference for lightskinned coloreds, we see the complex interplay of cultural and biological considerations that determines the status of Brazil's mestizo population. Social mobility in Brazil is a matter of both class and race.[20]

These refinements in the traditional interpretations of race relations in Brazil place comparative analyses in a new perspective. No longer does the United States look extraordinarily race-conscious in contrast to Brazil. Race prejudice is a significant factor in both countries, but the forms of prejudice appear to be much more subtle and complex in the Brazilian variant. Today's heightened awareness of the diverse dimensions of prejudice in Brazil gives a new twist to the comparison that makes the present-day situation appear more hopeful for the black man in the United States than for his counterpart in Brazil. The irony rests on the fact that the simplistic approach to prejudice and discrimination in the United States that identifies all people of color as "Negroes" has helped to generate a feeling of racial solidarity among blacks in their drive for better economic and social opportunities. This solidarity can be a precious psychological and political attribute.

The position of the mulatto in the two cultures well illustrates this point. In Brazil the mulatto can be cajoled into identifying himself with the well-established classes, a situation that drives a wedge between his own interests and those of the *negro* population. The well-accepted, successful Brazilian mulatto sees the black masses not as "brothers" but as a separate class of underprivileged pariahs. In contrast, the American taxonomy does not give parlance to the word "mulatto," although many American Negroes would be classified as mulattoes in Brazilian terms. Instead, prominent Americans of mixed racial heritage identify themselves as blacks and frequently speak out in behalf of the black community. In terms of class status or pigmentation, Thurgood Marshall, Edward Brooke, Roy Wilkins, and Julian Bond would be so well received as "conditional" whites in Brazilian society that it is reasonable to assume, had they been exposed to the Brazilian socialization process all of their lives, they might not have become associated with the blacks' cause.

American observers have often mistakenly interpreted the absence of a civil rights movement in Brazil as evidence of the lack of major race conflicts in the country. It would be closer to the truth to say that no broad-scale campaign for racial equality has arisen in Brazil because it would be extremely difficult to bring it about, given the fragmented racial loyalties of Brazil's colored population. The problems, frustrations, and discontent are there, but not racial solidarity. In the United States, however, few coloreds try to defect completely from the ranks of the "black" community. Recent interest in themes of Negritude, black nationalism, and black culture places added stress on tightening the bonds.[21] Though significant divisions exist within the black community on issues regarding economic programs, educational reform, political tactics, and violence, the general idea of demanding respect and equal opportunities without regard to color has clearly attracted widespread enthusiasm among American Negroes in recent decades. By joining hands to pressure society into tearing down its racial barriers, Afro-Americans have made significant strides toward improving their condition.

To some degree the fruits of this revolution in thought and action can be seen in the economic indices. In recent years the income gains of blacks in the United States have far outpaced the advances of blacks in Brazil. To be sure, much of this relative improvement can be traced to the faster and more comprehensive expansion of the American economy through developments in the consumer, defense, and service industries. But part of the change is also related to the demands for better opportunities placed on society by organized Afro-Americans. For example, when defense industries failed to show initiative in hiring unemployed blacks during the war mobilization of 1940 and 1941, A. Philip Randolph threatened to march on Washington with 50,000 to 100,000 protesters. The establishment of a Fair Employment Practices Commission as a response to this challenge fell short of its original promise, but it did help to place many blacks in war industry jobs. After World War II, the pace of improvement slowed; and, until the early 1960s, blacks did not make headway in closing the gap between their income and that of whites. But the situation began to improve in 1964 during the rising tide of the civil rights movement and increasing intellectual and social ferment in the black community. By the early 1970s blacks were closing the gap in white-black income, particularly in the category of young black northern couples with children. As the energy crisis and stagflation beset the country in the mid and late 1970s, the gap began to widen again. These disparities notwithstanding, many "working class" and middle-class blacks in the United States made substantial economic gains and enjoyed much greater income advancement than their Brazilian counterparts.[22] Black Brazilians have received some indirect economic dividends from their country's industrial growth since the 1930s, but the opportunities opened to them have largely been limited to marginal, temporary, or insecure jobs.[23] The frustrations of Abdias do Nascimento, an outspoken Afro-Brazilian who has tried to draw attention to the gains made through organized activity in the United States, attest to the difficulty of trying to stir enthusiasm for racial solidarity in Brazil.[24]

Ironically, then, the long history of blunt forms of racial discrimination in the United States sowed the seeds for an equally blunt attack on the prejudicial system; but the more complicated attitudes toward race and divided loyalties among colored groups in Brazil have made a frontal attack on prejudice a much more formidable task.

Lest students of race relations respond to the paradoxes of comparative study by becoming unduly optimistic about the prospects for racial justice in America, it should be noted that the implications of these new comparative perspectives can also be challenged. Is it possible, for example, that the system of racial identification in the United States is more complex than the two-category idea suggests and that therefore attitudes toward race in the United States and Brazil are not so different as commonly described? Should the lessons learned from reinterpreting Brazilian race relations caution us in reinterpreting American race relations? The answers to these questions seem to weigh heavily in the affirmative.

The preoccupation with "civil rights" and "black consciousness" in recent years has made the two-category system of race distinctions seem more rigid than it really has been. With a glut of new publications discussing the problems and demands of "The Negro" and a crisis between "blacks" and "whites," it is understandable that popular language has simplified the terms of historical discussion. Actually, the record is replete with evidence showing that a sliding scale of color prejudice has, to some degree, been in effect in the United States.

Generally speaking, through the course of American history lightskinned Negroes have fared better than darkskinned Negroes. During the days of slavery, for example, a disproportionate number of mulattoes worked in the more attractive positions as house servants, received the opportunities of manumission, and found places in the free colored population of the South.[25] With the demise of America's "peculiar institution," the light-colored group capitalized on its head start in acquiring education, skills, land, and capital and succeeded in moving into many of the positions of political leadership that opened to blacks during the Reconstruction Era. The predominance of light skins in the upper classes of black society continued into the twentieth century. Many became outstanding spokesmen for Negroes in their time—men such as Booker T. Washington and W. E. B. Du Bois.[26]

How did this happen? What explains the prominence of the lighter groups in the higher echelons vis-à-vis the concentration, until recently, of the more numerous darker individuals in the lower socioeconomic classes of the Negro community? Clearly part of the answer can be traced to the history of slavery. Many slave proprietors favored the children born from their sexual liaisons with bondswomen, giving these youngsters better opportunities than were available to the masses of slaves.[27] Color also seems to have been a very important factor. Masters were known to prefer lightskinned slaves for their sexual escapades.[28] Moreover, long after the passing of slavery, whites continued to express higher regard for mulattoes—an attitude that prevailed in spite of the growth of legal discrimination and the rising popularity of "scientific racism." Edward Reuter's book *The Mulatto in the United States*, published in 1917, reflected this attitude. Reuter looked askance at miscegenation and favored separation of the races, but he viewed mulattoes as mentally and culturally superior to darker-skinned Negroes. He believed mulattoes would fail in economic competition with whites and suffer great social discomfort if they tried to integrate into white society. By remaining active within the Negro caste, however, they could help calm racial tensions and provide valuable educational and leadership services for the darker masses.[29] When Horace R. Cayton and St. Clair Drake conducted an extensive study of race relations in Chicago in the 1940s, they encountered similar attitudes. The whites demanded racial "purity" and wanted mixed-bloods to remain with their own people, but whites also expressed the feeling that Caucasian blood could dilute some undesirable traits in cases of miscegenation, making the offspring more civilized. Mulattoes, quadroons, and octoroons were seen as a leavening force for the black community.[30]

It was one of the tragic conditions of the racial situation in the United States that many Negroes accepted the whites' value scale favoring "white" physical features. Through psychoanalysis, Abram Kardiner and Lionel Ovesey found several individuals trapped in a vicious circle of self-hatred because their compensatory measures to escape blackness proved futile. "Ugh, black is dirty, bad, no-good, evil!" exclaimed a woman who had been horrified and ashamed when she gave birth to two children who were much darker than herself or her husband.[31] Psychiatrists William H. Grier and Price M. Cobbs reviewed the painful frustration of efforts by black women to comb, plait, and press their hair, noting that "almost without exception black women in treatment recall that awful day when they first faced the swimming pool."[32] Studies by Kenneth Clark, W. Lloyd Warner, John Dollard, and Gunnar Myrdal well documented other dimensions of this syndrome.[33] Black children preferred white dolls;

black college students viewed light skin color as more aesthetically attractive than dark pigmentation; aspiring black individuals considered marriage to lightskinned partners valuable for their long-range career plans. With the premium on café au lait, mulattoes sometimes formed semiexclusive clubs and churches and condescended to the darker groups.[34] Gunnar Myrdal even found rabidly anti-Negro mulattoes.[35] There can be little doubt that the unfavorable self-image that this behavior created among darkskinned Negroes badly undermined self-confidence and, in some cases, caused severe personality difficulties.[36]

Out of America's own subtle sliding scale of racial values came a socioeconomic pattern that resembled the Brazilian situation in many ways. The American saying, "If your white, you're right; if your brown, stick around; if your black, step back!" would be understandable to many Brazilians regarding their own society.[37] Class profiles of the American Negro community drawn up in the 1940s usually placed lightskins in the upper economic ranks and charted an increasing proportion of darkskins with descending class positions.[38] This too resembles the Brazilian pattern. In fact, when interviewers asked lightskins to explain this condition, they often responded in ways similar to the comments of Brazilians. For example, one of W. Lloyd Warner's associates asked a fair-complexioned colored girl why there were no darkskins in her social clique. She explained that it was simply a matter of class; the darker groups did not have the means to move into her circle.[39]

Although this young lady may have harbored unconscious notions of color prejudice, her attention to class considerations certainly was not out of the ordinary. Attitudes about class status do represent an important component in social relations, including the specific area of race relations. It is significant that in recent years both blacks and whites in the United States have become less inclined to view dark color negatively. In the process, class considerations have become increasingly important in race relations.

In terms of black attitudes, it is clear that the ferment of civil rights and black consciousness activity stimulated a new sense of pride, confidence, and group solidarity. The psychological uplift created by these developments weakened in-group color prejudices. Since the 1940s many Afro-Americans have turned to a new priority list of values to assess individual status. The earlier, less flexible index of social worth that relied heavily on measuring the degree of "whiteness" in physical features has been replaced by criteria that focus greater attention on individual character and ability. Recent studies indicate that concern for wealth, education, and profession have surpassed preoccupation with skin color as prestige factors in the black community.[40]

White attitudes, too, have changed significantly in recent decades. Though many still suffer from the myopia of racial prejudice, a large segment of the white population has become increasingly aware of the inconsistencies between their society's historical treatment of blacks and the ideal of a system of justice unencumbered by racial discrimination. This new awareness is especially noticeable in the case of the younger generation. Compared to the 1940s, a much greater proportion of whites today is capable of dealing with blacks on the basis of individual merit rather than in terms of color-based status.[41]

As class considerations replace color considerations in the United States, the new pattern in race relations strangely begins to resemble the "traditional" interpretation of Brazilian society. By a different route, then, America has edged toward the Brazilian "ideal" in race relations. Instead of using the Brazilian approach in which the aggrieved groups try to *downplay* their color identity, blacks in the United States have worked to secure equal opportunities through a frontal assault on prejudice that *emphasizes* racial identity. Yet the American approach as stated in these simple terms is by no means a panacea. Assertion of race pride and unity may provide the political energy necessary to push the doors of opportunity ajar, but in the long run it cannot guarantee that many blacks will be able to capitalize on those opportunities. In a class-oriented society, racial solidarity alone will not suffice to expand opportunities greatly.

As the machinery of color discrimination is dismantled and the credentials of blacks are evaluated in class terms, deficiencies in such categories as vocational skills and higher education can prove to be weighty handicaps. Even if racism in the United States could be eradicated in a day, little elevation in the overall socioeconomic position of blacks would be likely without complementary expansion of opportunities that improve competitive qualifications in the job market.[42] Opportunities for greater residential mobility are important too, for, historically, the crowded, blighted, inner-city ghettoes have been breeding grounds for alienation and crime, whether populated by blacks or by whites.[43]

Thus, even "revisionist" interpretations of comparative race relations still reveal shortcomings and suggest problems that deserve further examination. Two points especially seem to warrant attention. The first relates to color. An understanding of the subtle forms of color prejudice in Brazil should remind us that historically, in the United States, too, lightskinned Afro-Americans have received more favorable treatment than darkskinned Afro-Americans. Although recent emphasis on black pride and solidarity has done much to undermine this value system, it would be naive to assume that it has been permanently destroyed. C. Eric Lincoln sounds an appropriate warning to both whites and blacks when he argues that "to say color is dead as an aspect of racial psychosis is to lay permanently to rest a troublesome syndrome likely to defy internment."[44]

The second point of caution regarding "revisionist" interpretations of comparative race relations concerns class. The modern-day penchant in the United States for exposing the evils of "racism" has diverted attention from a problem Brazilians have long recognized— that class stratification too can be a powerful social force in limiting mobility. Indeed, class prejudice can be just as restrictive and long-lasting as race prejudice, a fact that is evidenced by conditions in many Latin American countries.[45] In matters of race relations, class prejudice often serves to reinforce race prejudice.

A high view over the forest of interpretations and reinterpretations of comparative race relations concerning the United States and Brazil does produce at least one tenable conclusion that can be stated with confidence. The problems of color prejudice and class prejudice in the two societies are related, and the implications concerning the struggle for racial justice should be clear. Both problems must be challenged to bring meaningful change.

Notes

1. Gilberto Freyre, *New World in the Tropics: The Culture of Modern Brazil* (New York, 1959), p. 9.

2. Freyre presents many examples of racial prejudice in Brazil in his other works. *See*, for example, *The Mansions and the Shanties* (New York, 1963). For favorable interpretations of race relations in Brazil, *see* William Lytle Schurz, *This New World: The Civilization of Latin America* (New York, 1964), pp. 166–73; 390, 410, 412; Frank Tannenbaum, *Slave and Citizen: The Negro in the Americas* (New York, 1946); Robert Allen Christopher, "The Human Race in Brazil," *Americas* (July 1953), pp. 3–31. Similar in point of view but with more balanced interpretation of the problem of race prejudice are Artur Ramos, *The Negro in Brazil* (Washington, D.C., 1939); Donald Pierson, *Negroes in Brazil: A Study of Race Contact at Bahia* (Chicago, 1942).

3. For a summary of major ideas involved in the criticisms of "racial democracy," *see* Octavio Ianni, *Raças e classes sociais no Brasil* (Rio de Janeiro, 1966), pp. 3–72. Also, *see* Marvin Harris, *Patterns of Race in the Americas* (New York, 1964); Florestan Fernandes, *The Negro in Brazilian Society*, ed. Phyllis B. Eveleth and trans. Jacqueline D. Skiles, A. Brunel, and Arthur Rothwell (New York, 1969); Fernando Henrique Cardoso and Octávio Ianni, *Côr e mobilidade em Florianopolis: Aspectos das relações êntre negros e brancos numa communidade do Brasil meridional* (São Paulo, 1960); Oracy Nogueira, "Skin Color and Social Class," in *Plantation Systems of the New World* (Washington, D.C., 1959). Thomas G. Sanders offers interesting critical commentary based on personal observation in "The Social Functions of Futebol," *American Universities Field Staff, Inc.: East Coast South America Series* 14 no. 2 (1970). Among the important recent comparative studies are: Carl N. Degler, *Neither Black Nor White: Slavery and Race Relations in Brazil and the United States* (New York, 1971); Harry Hoetink, *Slavery and Race Relations in the Americas* (New York, 1973); Harry Hoetink, *Two Variants in Caribbean Race Relations* (New York, 1971); Ann M. Pescatello, ed., *Old Roots in New Lands: Historical and Anthropological Perspectives on Black Experiences in the Americas* (Westport, Conn., 1977). For criticisms of the "myth" of racial democracy in Brazil, *see* Thomas E. Skidmore, *Black into White: Race and Nationality in Brazilian Thought* (New York, 1974), and Robert Brent Toplin, ed., *Slavery and Race Relations in Latin America* (Westport, Conn., 1974).

4. Christopher, "The Human Race in Brazil." Charles Wagley summarizes this view but also presents penetrating criticisms of it in *An Introduction to Brazil* (New York, 1963), pp. 132–47.

5. Two books give particularly good reviews of the history of the "closed" system in post-Civil War America: C. Van Woodward, *The Strange Career of Jim Crow*, rev. ed. (London, 1966), pp. 67–147; Allen Weinstein and Frank Otto Gatell, *The Segregation Era, 1863–1954: A Modern Reader* (New York, 1970).

6. *See,* for example, the comments in the introduction to the section on "Race and Economics" in Joanne Grant, ed., *Black Protest: History, Documents, and Analyses, 1619 to the Present* (New York, 1968), 426-32; Malcom X, *The Autobiography of Malcolm X* (New York, 1966), p. 284.

7. Marvin Harris, "Racial Identity in Brazil," *Luso-Brazilian Review* (Winter 1964), pp. 21-28. Harris' own views are, in many respects, critical of the "traditional" interpretation.

8. Gilberto Freyre is most prominently associated with the thesis that Brazil's heterogeneous racial population can be traced to the liberal attitudes of Portuguese settlers toward interracial unions. *See,* especially, *The Masters and the Slaves* (New York, 1956). Magnus Mörner summarizes some of the research on this subject in *Race Mixture in the History of Latin America* (Boston, 1967). It is clear that Brazilians were more tolerant of interracial sexual relations than Americans, especially in terms of attitudes toward miscegenation as reflected in law. During times of slavery, many of the American colonies (and later the states) explicitly prohibited miscegenation. There is no evidence of such widespread legal interference with interracial unions in Brazil. A distinction should be made between law and practice however, since miscegenation occurred extensively in both societies. As James Hugo Johnston concludes in a study of antebellum Virginia, "The law did little to prevent miscegenation, and this subject must be considered a question of human, not of legal, relations." *See, Race Relations in Virginia and Miscegenation in the South: 1776-1860* (Amherst, Mass., 1970), pp. 313-14. Also, *see* Winthrop D. Jordan, *White Over Black: American Attitudes Toward the Negro, 1550-1812* (Baltimore, 1969), pp. 136-42.

9. Frank Tannenbaum, *Ten Keys to Latin America* (New York, 1964), pp. 112-13.

10. Marvin Harris identifies the American pattern of calling anyone who is known to have Negro ancestry a Negro "the rule of hypo-descent." *See, Patterns of Race in the Americas* (New York, 1964), p. 56. As James Bryce summarized the contrast tersely, "In Latin America whoever is not black is white; in teutonic America whoever is not white is black." *See, The American Commonwealth* (New York, 1910), p. 555.

11. James Weldon Johnson's *The Autobiography of an Ex-Colored Man* (New York, 1927), a novel, remains one of the most fascinating works written on the phenomenon of "passing" in American society. Johnson first published the book anonymously in 1912.

12. Florestan Fernandes, *A integração do negro na sociedade de classes,* 2 vols. (São Paulo, 1965), I: 26-37, 41-43; Carl N. Degler, "The Negro in America: Where Myrdal Went Wrong," *The New York Times Magazine,* December 7, 1969, pp. 157-60.

13. *See,* for example, Pierson, *Negroes in Brazil,* p. 177.

14. C. R. Boxer, *The Golden Age of Brazil, 1695-1750* (Berkeley and Los Angeles, 1963); Stanley J. Stein, *Vassouras, A Brazilian Coffee County 1850-1900* (Cambridge, 1957); Emília Viotti da Costa, *Da senzala à colônia* (São Paulo, 1966); Octávio Ianni, *As metamorfoses do escravo: Apogeu e crise da escravatura no Brasil Meridional* (São Paulo, 1962); Robert Brent Toplin, "From Slavery to Fettered Freedom: Attitudes Toward the Negro in Brazil," *Luso-Brazilian Review* (Summer 1970), pp. 3-12.

15. Fernandes, *A integração do negro na sociedade de classes*, I: 1-69; Abdias do Nascimento et al., *O negro brasileiro: 80 anos de abolição* (Rio de Janeiro, 1968); "80 anos de abolição," *Cadernos Brasileiros* (May-June 1968); Abdias do Nascimento, *O Negro revoltado* (Rio de Janeiro, 1968), pp. 15-82.

16. Florestan Fernandes, "Imagração e relaçãoes raciais," *Revista Civilisação Brasileira* 8 (1966), pp. 75-96; Thomas E. Skidmore, "Brazilian Intellectuals and the Problem of Race, 1870-1930," *The Graduate Center for Latin American Studies*, Occasional Paper No. 6. Brazilian writers interested in the Negro exhibited these prejudices in the postemancipation period. *See* Oliveira Vianna, *Evolução do povo brasileiro*, 2d ed. (São Paulo, 1933), p. 156; Nina Rodrigues, *Os africanos no Brasil*, 3d ed (São Paulo, 1945).

17. Harry Hoetink, *The Two Variants in Caribbean Race Relations: A Contribution to the Sociology of Segmented Societies* (London, 1967), pp. 120-22.

18. Michael Banton, *Race Relations* (New York, 1967), pp. 280-81. For an insightful discussion of attitudes toward mulattoes and other groups in northern Brazil, *see* Charles Wagley, *Amazon Town: A Study of Man in the Tropics* (New York, 1964), pp. 128-44.

19. Charles Wagley, "Plantation America: A Culture Sphere," in Vera Rubin, ed., *Caribbean Studies: A Symposium* (Seattle, 1960), pp. 7-8. Thomas B. Skidmore and Carl N. Degler commented on the implications of this information for comparative interpretations in the conference on "Comparative Race Relations Since Emancipation: The United States and Other Countries," 36th Annual Meeting of the Southern Historical Association, November 12, 1970.

20. Scholars interested in comparative study of the relationship between attitudes toward race and class should see Eugene D. Genovese, *The World the Slaveholders Made: Two Essays in Interpretation* (New York, 1969), pp. 103-13 Magnus Mörner, (ed), *Race and Class in Latin America* (New York, 1970), pp. 1-8; J. H. Plumb, "Poverty and Race," *The New York Review of Books*, March 13, 1969, pp. 3-5.

21. St. Clair Drake, "Hide My Face?: On Pan-Africanism and Negritude," in Herbert Hill, ed., *Soon, One Morning* (New York, 1963), pp. 100-05.

22. U.S. Department of Commerce, *Statistical Abstract of the United*

States: 1978 (Washington, D.C., 1978), pp. 457-60; U.S. Bureau of the Census, Current Population Reports, Series P-60, Np. 66, "Income in 1968 of Families and Persons in the United States " (Washington, D.C., 1969); The New York Times, February 12, 1971, pp. 1, 24; Arthur M. Ross, "The Negro in the American Economy," and Vivian W. Henderson, "Regions, Race, and Jobs," in Arthur M. Ross and Herbert Hill, eds., Employment, Race, and Poverty (New York, 1967), pp. 13–20, 38, 46, 87–91. It should be pointed out, however, that despite gains in black family and individual incomes relative to white family and individual incomes, the absolute dollar difference between the two groups has been increasing. Also, the 1970 census shows little or no significant improvement relative to whites in such categories as black families with no father present, older black families in the North and West, and all types of black families in the South.

23. Roger Bastide, "The Development of Race Relations in Brazil," in Guy Hunter, ed., Industrialization and Race Relations: A Symposium (London, 1965), pp. 19–21.

24. Nascimento et al., O negro brasileiro, pp. 63, 72–90; Nascimento, O negro revoltado, pp. 15–82.

25. Charles S. Sydnor, "The Free Negro in Mississippi Before the Civil War," American Historical Review (July 1927), pp. 787–88; Frederick Law Olmstead, The Slave States, ed. with an introductory essay by Harvey Wish (New York, 1959), p. 89; Forrest G. Wood, Black Scare: The Racist Response to Emancipation and Reconstruction (Berkeley, 1970), p. 70.

26. Ray Stannard Baker, Following the Color Line, Harper Torchbook edition (New York, 1964), pp. 155–57; W. Lloyd Warner, Buford H. Junker, and Walter A. Adams, Color and Human Nature: Negro Personality Development in a Northern City (Washington, D.C., 1941), pp. 192, 195; Howard E. Freeman, David Armor, J. Michael Ross, and Thomas F. Pettigrew, "Color Gradation and Attitudes Among Middle-Income Negroes," American Sociological Review (June 1966), p. 366.

27. J. Merton England, "The Free Negro in Ante-Bellum Tennessee," The Journal of Southern History (February 1943), p. 43; John H. Russell, The Free Negro in Virginia: 1619-1865 (New York, 1969), p. 127; Frederick Douglass, Life and Times of Frederick Douglass (New York, 1969), pp. 62–63; Sydnor, "The Free Negro in Mississippi Before the Civil War," pp. 787–88; Warner et al., Color and Human Nature, p. 170.

28. Kenneth M. Stampp, The Peculiar Institution: Slavery in the Ante-Bellum South (New York, 1956), p. 259; Richard C. Wade, Slavery in the Cities: The South, 1820-1860 (London 1964), pp. 122–23; Wood, Black Scare, p. 70.

29. Edward Byron Reuter, *The Mulatto in the United States, Including a Study of the Role of Mixed-Blood Races Throughout the World* (Boston, 1918), pp. 340, 358–79, 391–95.

30. St. Clair Drake and Horace R. Cayton, *Black Metropolis: A Study of Negro Life in a Northern City* (New York, 1945), pp. 268–69. For other examples of white preference for lightskin Negroes over darkskin Negroes, see John Dollard, *Caste and Class in a Southern Town* (New Haven, 1937), pp. 71, 92–93; Warner et al., *Color and Human Nature*, p. 171. Also, see John G. Mencke, *Mulattoes and Race Mixture: American Attitudes and Images, 1865–1918* (Ann Arbor, Mich., 1979).

31. Abram Kardiner and Lionel Ovesey, *The Mark of Oppression: Explorations in the Personality of the American Negro* (Cleveland 1951), pp. 135–36, 155, 187–88, 190, 233, 252–57, 286–92, 315–16.

32. William H. Grier and Price M. Cobbs, *Black Rage* (New York, 1968), pp. 40–52, 54, 79–80.

33. Kenneth B. Clark and Mamie P. Clark, "Racial Identification and Preference in Negro Children," in Eleanor E. Maccoley, Theodore M. Newcomb, and Eugene D. Hartley, *Readings in Social Psychology* (New York, 1947), pp. 602–11; W. B. Burghardt Du Bois, *Dusk of Dawn: An Essay Toward an Autobiography of a Race Concept* (New York, 1940), p. 179; Allison Dais, Burleigh B. Gardner, and Mary R. Gardner, *Deep South : A Social Anthropological Study of Caste and Class* (Chicago, 1941), pp. 244–48; Gunnar Myrdal, with the assistance of Richard Sterner and Arnold Rose, *An American Dilemma: The Negro Problem and Modern Democracy* (New York, 1944), p. 686; Freeman et al., "Color Gradation and Attitudes Among Middle Income Negroes, p. 365; Warner et al., *Color and Human Nature,* pp. 1, 14, 16–19, 169–71, 197–99; Dollard, *Caste and Class in a Southern Town*, p. 68.

34. Du Bois, *Dusk of Dawn*, p. 188; Myrdal, *An American Dilemma*, p. 696; Warner et al., *Color and Human Nature* p. 196; E. Franklin Frazier, *Black Bourgeoisie* (Glencoe, 1957), pp. 113–14, 137.

35. Myrdal, *An American Dilemma*, p. 699.

36. St. Clair Drake, "The Social and Economic Status of the Negro in the United States," *Daedalus* (Fall 1965), p. 801; Warner et al., *Color and Human Nature*, pp. 6, 292.

37. Freeman et al., "Color Gradation and Attitudes Among Middle-Income Negroes," p. 365.

38. The terms "lightskin" and "darkskin" used in this section are based on the word usage of W. Lloyd Warner and his associates. Warner et al., *Color and Human Nature*, pp. 27, 293; Du Bois, *Dusk of Dawn*, pp. 179–82; Myrdal, *An American Dilemma*, p. 131.

39. Warner et al., *Color and Human Nature*, p. 209. Marcus Garvey's Universal Negro Improvement Association and his emphasis on blackness drew much support from the lower-class masses of darkskin Negroes who were disgusted not only with the treatment they received from whites but also with the aloofness of many lightskin middle- and upper-class Negroes. B. David Cronon, *Black Moses: The Story of Marcus Garvey* (Madison, 1955), pp. 39–72.

40. C. Eric Lincoln, "Color and Group Identity in the United States," in John Hope Franklin, ed., *Color and Race* (Boston, 1968), pp. 253–54, 258; Norval D. Glenn, "Negro Prestige Criteria: A Case Study in the Bases of Prestige," *American Journal of Sociology* (May 1963), 645–57; Freeman et al., "Color Gradation and Attitudes Among Middle-Income Negroes," pp. 366, 373.

41. William Brink and Louis Harris, *Black and White: A Study of U.S. Racial Attitudes Today* (New York, 1967), pp. 124–27; *New York Times*, February 4 and 21, 1979.

42. Tobe Johnson offered an insightful discussion of this matter with regard to black studies programs in "Black Studies: Their Origins, Present State, and Prospects," revised and expanded version of a paper read before the American Conference of Academic Deans, Pittsburgh, Pennsylvania, January 13, 1969.

43. *See*, for example, the letter from Milton S. Eisenhower, former chairman of the National Commission on the Causes and Prevention of Violence, in *Harper's* (December 1970), pp. 6–10.

44. Lincoln, "Color and Group Identity in the United States," pp. 254, 257.

45. Tannenbaum, *Ten Keys to Latin America*, pp. 49–52.

The Problem of Double Identity:
Black Brazilians on the Issue
of Racial Consciousness*

North American progress toward civil rights has made an emotional impact on Brazilian society and stirred Afro-Americans to reconsider familiar questions about the best way to seek equality. They ask: Is class discrimination the primary barrier to opportunity? Or is color discrimination the real obstacle? In the context of North America's assault against racial inequality many Brazilians have been giving greater emphasis to the second factor by exposing the subtle but significant forms of color discrimination in their society.

The debate over this issue resembles, in many ways, the question about "twoness" addressed by W. E. B DuBois many years ago. The feeling is not limited to blacks in the United States. In Brazil, too, where Negroes represent a minority of the national population, the black man continues to face the vexing question: "Who am I?" He must decide whether to place greater emphasis on the first or the second part of his hyphenated identity as an Afro-Brazilian. He may choose between viewing himself in terms of economic class or in terms of color grouping. Undoubtably, many feel within themselves the pull of forces of allegiance: the desire to be integrated as Brazilians without class discrimination and the interest in affirming their black identity. Coming to grips with this problem has been especially

---

*An earlier version of "The Problem of Double Identity: Black Brazilians on the Issue of Racial Consciousness" by the author appeared in *Black World* (1972) and the revised form is reprinted by permission of BLACK WORLD magazine copyright 1972 by Johnson Publishing Company, Inc.

difficult in a period of increasing group consciousness, a time when some Afro-Brazilians are raising serious questions about the realities of racial prejudice and discrimination in their country.

Although the myth of "racial paradise" in Brazil is gradually losing credibility, its decline in popularity hardly simplifies the choices black Brazilians must make in defining the future course of their struggle for equality.[1] Just as in the United States, where the ferment of social protest has excited significant disagreements about ideology and strategy, black Brazilians too differ in diagnosing problems and prescribing remedies. These differences came out dramatically during a roundtable discussion in Rio de Janeiro on March 4, 1968, when a group of outstanding black Brazilian intellectuals assembled to assess the position of Afro-Brazilians eighty years after the abolition of slavery.[2] The opinions they expressed highlighted some of the central questions concerning equality-conscious blacks in Brazil today.[3] Significantly, in many respects these questions resemble the issues that divide Afro-Americans in the United States.

Participants in the conference were extraordinarily candid and penetrating in explaining their professional understanding of the state of race relations and describing their own personal experiences. They pointed out sizeable gaps between the theory and practice of "racial democracy" and questioned Brazil's reputation for being an unusually tolerant society. Cataloguing a long list of examples to illustrate the prevalence of discrimination in schools, hotels, theatres, factories, the medical profession, the military, and even Brazil's Foreign Ministry, the group painted a gloomy portrait of the barriers facing darkskinned Brazilians. Some attributed the inequality in treatment to "racism"; others suggested that the legacy of slavery—the continued low economic and social status of the majority of the black community since the time of emancipation—was at the root of the problem.[4]

The participants also stressed the difficulties Afro-Brazilians incur when they try to expose cases of prejudice. One of the discussants, Sebastião Rodrigues Alves, noted that when blacks complained about discrimination, whites frequently referred to a clause in the national Constitution stating that all the people were equal before the law. "It [the clause] is a beautiful thing," said Rodrigues Alves, "but, in reality, we know that the Negro is relegated to a situation of social inferiority and every time that he rises up against the state of things he is taken as subversive, as audacious, and, particularly, as a Negro racist." Rodrigues Alves thought improvement in race relations would be difficult until whites recognized the reality of prejudice and their own culpability in the discriminatory system.[5] In a comment that rang like a statement from the Kerner Commission Report, he asserted, "The Negro's problem is the white's problem. It is the white who created the Negro's problem."[6]

During the course of discussion, ideas gradually diverged as two very prominent figures, Edison Carneiro and Abdias do Nascimento, moved to the forefront of debate. Carneiro is a respected ethnologist and the author of several scholarly studies on African cults and folklore in Brazil and the history of Brazilian Negroes. Nascimento, a leader of the Experimental Negro Theatre in the 1940s and an active writer and lecturer, is particularly interested in the self-consciousness of blacks in Brazil.[7]

A heated forensic duel between the two began when the moderator asked: "Is it possible to diagnose a specifically Negro culture in present-day Brazil of African origin or of enduring, on-going universality?" Carneiro contended that Brazil's long history of colonial domination by the Portuguese and the experience of slavery destroyed most aspects of African cultural heritage. *Some* traces of African culture were still evident in modern times, he admitted, but they were few and, in many cases, had become integrated into Brazil's national culture. Carneiro reviewed the history of *samba* as a case in point. Origins of the dance and music could be traced to Angola, he explained, but the tradition of mass-participation in samba dances organized by "schools" of samba that plan elaborate choreography is a Brazilian rather than an African development. In modern times the samba is not a monopoly of blacks; whites, too, engage in the dances and music and make their own contributions to the samba tradition. As in the history of samba, so in the case of other African legacies, explained Carneiro. Each day the black is losing his ties with Africa and becoming more and more a "naturalized" Brazilian.[8]

Nascimento registered an angry protest against what he described as the idea that, historically, whites had succeeded in wiping out black culture in Brazil. Negro culture had not completely "disappeared," Nascimento insisted. Black values and cultural identification were recognized not only in Africa but throughout the Americas where "Afro-Americans" lived. After all, how could one explain the widespread interest in Negritude, he asked? Nascimento contended that the idea of Negritude represented a force of collective identification that offered cultural redemption.[9]

When Carneiro and Nascimento finally addressed themselves to the question of how black Brazilians should combat the problem of racial discrimination, the issues of the debate broadened into a full-blown discussion of strategy and tactics. Their own words best communicate the significance and the emotional impact of their disagreements in interpretation:[10]

Abdias Do Nascimento: I think that if Brazil is to be truly democratic it has to give the Negro a chance to be present in all the social classes, not just the working class and the wretched class. The Negro should be present in all the classes including the elite directing classes, because there, yes there, we should really have racial democracy. And he should especially be present in the cultural organs where one would assume there is great toleration, broad understanding, and considerable airing of views in relation to all kinds of problems. It is due to this situation that I want to say that in this problem of suppressing cultures we cannot continue putting up with inactive and passive people who go on accepting the situation. The Negro has to take a position . . . [Heated exchange between Nascimento and Carneiro makes recording impossible].

Edison Carneiro: [Later, referring back to Nascimento's comments] I do not understand these questions about prejudice. It is a problem that has always displeased me because prejudice is always based on emotions that undoubtedly have an immediate origin which is sometimes brutal and violent. But whatever the reason for it, prejudice is based on emotions that require the attention of a psychologist more than an ethnologist like myself. It never interested me as a theme of study. I do have the impression that people are moving toward an unfortunate perspective, and that prejudice is increasingly rising in Brazil. The facts presented at this meeting are, naturally, a little old, but they do show that we have a type of society that promotes prejudice. We are also in a period of Brazilian life in which there is great economic development. The development of the country— and development can be as much forward as backward—the fact is that the country is growing, is experimenting with its potential in various fields, and all this is going to create much more prejudice than we have today. To the extent that the black man becomes educated and earns money and respect, he becomes more the target of prejudice than before. Until a short time ago the Negro would not compete with the white. He had that thing which Abdias do Nascimento described very well: he knew his place. Today, the black does not know "his place," and, as he begins to compete with the white, the inevitable occurs. As a consequence, prejudice is going to grow. On the other hand, external factors are also significant: the imitation of the United States, which appears to be the standard, the model for a great number of imbeciles we have in this country and for other people who simply want to make money. The examples of other countries are relevant too, like South Africa or the idea that some Brazilians still hold from the time of Nazism when it was maintained that certain races and certain people were responsible for the evils of the world. People who think in this manner will create much more prejudice in Brazil than we presently have. We must be prepared for that. I do not believe that such preparation should be made in the sense of speaking about ourselves specifically as Negroes and creating Negro organizations, etc., because that contributes one more factor to prejudice, one more factor to conflict. On the contrary, to the degree that the Negro fights arm in arm with the Brazilian people, as Brazilian people, against the injustices, against the baseness, against the distortions of civilized life, so much greater will be the possibility of combating prejudices. In other words, an isolated movement of Negroes of the type you mentioned, such as the Negro Front" and the "Negro Legion," will fail, while if the Negro participates in the general movement of the Brazilian people, for his economic betterment, out of respect for his individual rights, through a better constitution, through the better distribution of wealth in Brazil, then we will certainly have a diminution of prejudice.

Sebastião Rodrigues Alves: If the Negro exists, he cannot negate himself. He will not gain anything at all by trying to hide his existence.

Edison Carneiro: Black is the specific coloration of a group in the human species. We are all the same thing. Let's put aside that other nonsense. All of us are of the same human species, we are the human species. Don't put things in individual terms. If a white comes to insult me, the only thing to do is resist and slap him in the face, but in national terms no isolated group will be able to do anything. We have the example now of the "milis" who were able to form a little club for themselves, but that is a privileged class in Brazil. Outside of that, all other Brazilians will either unite together or they will be liquidated, to put it simply. If the negro is a part of the Brazilian people. . . . When one speaks of the Brazilian people it is good to explain that. . . . There was a French revolutionary who said the following: "Who are the people? The people are all the population, less their exploiters." If those who are not exploiters unite together and fight for their rights, for their well-being, for the progress of the country, for better organization of Brazilian life, for better distribution of Brazilian wealth, we have many more chances not only for a better way of life but also to destroy prejudice [excited exchange of comments as participants attempt to refute opinion of Edison Carneiro].

I am giving my opinion. The problem is this: if the black and his descendants, as was said here, are twenty million in a national population of eighty million, we have sixty million that are not Negroes. Don't these other sixty million want good food? Don't they want good housing? Don't they want a better political situation? As part of the people we can get very much. It is in that way that we can do something. Perhaps what the Negro is doing in the United States is right, because the Negro in the United States is in a much worse situation than here. In the

United States he isn't equal. Among other things, you can read, if you want, a book that is in all the libraries called *Escolha as minhas armas*, which tells of the case of a Negro in the United States who had broken his arm in an automobile accident with a university professor, also a Negro. When they arrived at a gasoline station, there is a white rascal standing at the entrance, and the Negro is afraid to blow the horn or move the car forward because the white is there. The other Negro— who writes the book—who is from a different section of the country, says:

"What the hell! Run the car over that guy!" And the other, frightened, cries:

"No, no! . . ."

After a long time, some twenty minutes, the white fellow turns and says:

"Hey, Negro, what do you want? Do you want gas for your car? Pull in."

So the Negro pulls in and says:

"Put in twenty liters."

And the gas station attendant answers him:

"But this piece of junk can take forty liters. Let's put in forty liters."

The Negro did not have the courage to resist or even to speak, so the white guy put in forty liters. Would that ever happen in Brazil—any place? Something like that? Then the situation is worse there.

Sebastião Rodrigues Alves: When it happens that a Negro arrives at a meeting like this of Negroes reflecting on their own problems and prospects and one from the group says that the Negro's problem is diluted or is involved in the problem of the people, I think the situation here is much worse than it is in the United States.

Edison Carneiro: That's your opinion. The fact is that the Negro is one of the people and the Negro has to move forward as the people; he cannot move against them.

Abdias Do Nascimento: Actually he is one of the people, but the solution to the people's problem alone does not resolve the Negro's problem. There are implications, obviously, but it is to falsify, to distort the problem, to think that we will resolve the problem of the people without giving conscience to the race, to the color, of the Negro. No, it is not resolved! . . . Because the integration of the Negro does not mean there is no disrespect for his personality. I agree that the Negro is not divorced from and cannot be alien to the problems of Brazilians in general, that's clear. What I want to say is that he has specific problems, and that to omit or to make these problems secondary is a reactionary attitude, because it obstructs precisely that matter of conscience and that position of the Negro that is fundamental not only for his elevation in status but also for his specific vindication. Otherwise, the Negro remains dissolved among the Brazilian people as a purely marginal and parasitic element.

Edison Carneiro: It appears that we are speaking two different languages. What I said was only this: the Negro is part of the Brazilian people. Then, by the way in which he fights with the Brazilian people for better conditions of life, for better health conditions, for better distribution of wealth. . . .

Abdias Do Nascimento: When I founded the Experimental Negro Theatre there were all kinds of popular movements, including those called "popular centers of culture." Meanwhile, the Negro was always excluded and discriminated against, never having real opportunities. Opportunities only developed after the Negro took the initiative to organize his own theatre movement. And the Negro theatre was not absolutely segregated. The negro was in touch with all the popular trends while, at the same time, he was affirming his own characteristics and holding open his own prospects.

Edison Carneiro: I am not saying that. . . .

Abdias Do Nascimento: Negro organizations are necessary because you will not get anywhere thinking that rights are conceded. Rights are taken; they are the fruit of a struggle!

To a certain degree, both Carneiro and Nascimento offered valid commentary on the task of improving race relations in Brazil even though at first glance their contradictory analyses would seem to complicate efforts to understand conditions as they now stand and to map out an effective strategy for change in the future. Abdias do Nascimento underscored the reality of racial prejudice in Brazil, a condition that will not disappear simply by ignoring it or downplaying its importance. If prejudice and discrimination against blacks as a group can operate independently of prejudice and discrimination against Brazilian poor people in general, then assertion of power *by* blacks *as* blacks will be necessary in the drive for equal treatment and opportunity. Collective action through group pride and awareness of cultural heritage seems to be a sine qua non for meaningful change. On the other hand, Edison Carneiro points out another important dimension by noting that the problems of Brazil's masses cut across racial lines. Indeed, in Brazil as well as in the United States there are many facets of the story of social and economic exploitation that are not simply a product of racial attitudes. If the plight of the masses, including nonblacks, is connected to the total scheme of things, a Portuguese language version of "United we stand; divided we fall" may hold some truth. In short, the future of the black Brazilian is tied up not only with the fate of his dark-skinned brothers but also with the future of all of Brazil's discontented masses.

Notes

1. As popularly understood, the "myth" described Brazilian society as extraordinarily tolerant in attitudes toward race (especially in contrast to society in the United States). Among the examples frequently used to support this thesis were the high incidence of miscegenation, the absence of government-sanctioned discrimination and a flexible attitude exhibited by Brazilians that recognized many different color categories and, in assessing the status of individuals, gave greater emphasis to class position than to color. Numerous studies have appeared in recent years to refute this interpretation. In Brazil sociologist Florestan Fernandes is most notably associated with the new views. One of his major works now appears in English: *The Negro in Brazilian Society*, edited by Phyllis B. Eveleth and translated by Jacqueline D. Skiles, A. Brunel, and Arthur Rothwell (New York, 1969). The studies of Fernandes' students such as Fernando Henrique Cardoso, Octavio Ianni, and Emília Viotti da Costa are also important. Among the works in English which develop and summarize some of the new views are: Marvin Harris,

Patterns of Race in the Americas (New York, 1964); Magnus Mörner, *Race Mixture in the History of Latin America* (Boston, 1967); H. Hoetink, *The Two Variants in Caribbean Race Relations: A Contribution to the Sociology of Segmented Societies* (London, 1967); Michael Banton, *Race Relations* (New York, 1967); Carl N. Degler, *Neither Black Nor White: Slavery and Race Relations in Brazil and the United States* (New York, 1971).

2. Brazil abolished slavery on May 13, 1888. For details on the causes of abolition, *see* Richard Graham, "Causes for the Abolition of Negro Slavery in Brazil: An Interpretive Essay," *Hispanic American Historical Review* (May 1966), pp. 123–37; Robert Brent Toplin, "Upheaval, Violence, and the Abolition of Slavery in Brazil: The Case of São Paulo," *Hispanic American Historical Review* (November 1969), pp. 639–55.

3. *80 Anos de abolição: O negro brasileiro* (Rio de Janeiro, 1968), published by the journal *Cadernos Brasileiros*. The journal also published a special issue on the topic of "The Brazilian Negro Eighty Years After the Abolition of Slavery" in May-June 1968.

4. For an interpretation of the connection between racism and the legacy of slavery, *see* Robert Brent Toplin, "From Slavery to Fettered Freedom: Attitudes Toward the Negro in Brazil," *Luso-Brazilian Review* (Summer 1970), pp. 3–12.

5. *80 Anos de abolição*, pp. 24-25. In view of the context of the discussion, I have translated the Portuguese word *negro* as "Negro."

6. Rodrigues Alves' statement resembles the conclusion of the Commission that, "What white Americans have never fully understood—but what the Negro can never forget—is that white society is deeply implicated in the ghetto. White institutions created it, white institutions maintain it, and white society condones it." *Report of tne National Advisory Commission on Civil Disorders* (New York, 1968), p. 2.

7. For examples of their writings, *see* Abdias do Nascimento, *O negro revoltado* (Rio de Janeiro, 1968); Edison Carneiro, *Os cultos de origem africana no Brasil* (Rio de Janeiro, 1959); Edison Carneiro, *Ladinos e crioulos: Estudos sôbre o negro no Brasil* (Rio de Janeiro, 1964); Edison Carneiro, *O quilombo dos Palmares*, 3rd ed. (Rio de Janeiro, 1966).

8. *80 Anos da abolição*, pp. 58-61.

9. Ibid., pp. 63–64.

10. The following text is translated from pages 73, 83-89 of *80 Anos de abolição*. The author is indebted to Vicente Barretto, editor of *Cadernos Brasileiros*, for permission to translate and publish the transcript of the debate.

11. By "nonblacks" I am referring not only to whites but also to mulattoes who, in Brazilian society, often view themselves as distinct from the Negro population.

Selected Bibliography

The literature of slavery and race relations in the United States and Brazil has been growing fast, especially since Frank Tannenbaum's little book, *Slave and Citizen: The Negro in the Americas* (New York: Vintage, 1946) dramatically compared the two societies and helped create a revolution in scholarship. The following bibliography does not attempt to present a complete survey of the vast literature on the subject; rather, it identifies some of the principal secondary works useful for a review of changing interpretations.

Several important comparative studies of slavery and race relations in the Americas have appeared in recent years. Magnus Mörner gives a broad survey of the historical issues in *Race Mixture in the History of Latin America* (Boston: Little, Brown, 1967), and Michael Banton stresses sociological perspectives and a global comparison in *Race Relations* (London: Basic Books, 1967). Sociological models are also the interest of Pierre L. Van den Berghe, who describes paternalistic and competitive societies in *Race and Racism: A Comparative Perspective* (New York: Wiley, 1967). Van den Berghe's approach is challenged in H. Hoetink, *Slavery and Race Relations in the Americas: Comparative Notes on Their Nature and Nexus* (New York: Oxford, 1973). Hoetink's earlier work, *Caribbean Race Relations: A Study of Two Variants* (New York: Oxford, 1971), explores the concept of the "somatic norm image" and is also a major contribution to the debate. Marvin Harris stresses economic factors in attacking "myths" about friendly masters and friendly race relations in *Patterns of Race in the Americas* (New York: Walker, 1964), and Carl N. Degler offers the best specific comparison of the U.S. and Brazil in *Neither Black Nor White: Slavery and Race Relations in Brazil and the United States* (New York: Macmillan, 1971). Among the anthologies on Latin America that offer intriguing ideas for comparative study are: Magnus Mörner, ed., *Race and Class in Latin America* (New York:

Columbia University, 1970); Robert Brent Toplin, ed., *Slavery and Race Relations in Latin America* (Westport, Conn.: Greenwood, 1974); Ann M. Pescatello, *The African in Latin America* (New York: Random House, 1975); Ann M. Pescatello, *Old Roots in New Lands: Historical and Anthropological Perspectives on Black Experiences in the Americas* (Westport, Conn.: Greenwood, 1977).

The subject of comparative slavery has excited much imaginative research. Stanley Elkins stirred considerable debate by expanding Tannenbaum's thesis in *Slavery: A Problem in American Institutional and Intellectual Life* (Chicago: University of Chicago, 1959). Major criticisms of Elkins are reviewed in Ann J. Lane, *The Debate over Slavery: Stanley Elkins and His Critics* (Urbana: University of Illinois, 1971). David Brion Davis implicitly questions many of Tannenbaum's assumptions in two large and impressive studies: *The Problem of Slavery in Western Culture* (Ithaca: Cornell University, 1966) and *The Problem of Slavery in the Age of Revolution, 1770–1823* (Ithaca: Cornell University, 1975). Eugene D. Genovese discusses the lessons of a U.S.-Brazil comparison in *The World the Slaveholders Made: Two Essays in Interpretation* (New York: Random House, 1969). Specific issues about comparative slavery are examined in Eugene D. Genovese and Lauria Foner, eds., *Slavery in the New World* (Englewood Cliffs: Prentice-Hall, 1969); Eugene D. Genovese and Stanley L. Engerman, eds., *Race and Slavery in the Western Hemisphere: Quantitative Studies* (Princeton: Princeton University, 1975); and C. Duncan Rice, *The Rise and Fall of Black Slavery* (New York: Harper and Row, 1975). The status of freedmen in the Americas is broadly examined in David Cohen and Jack P. Greene, eds., *Neither Slave Nor Free* (Baltimore: Johns Hopkins University, 1972).

There is an abundance of excellent secondary works on slavery in the United States. A standard place to begin is Kenneth M. Stampp's major study, *The Peculiar Institution: Slavery in the Ante-Bellum South* (New York: Random House, 1956). Since the publication of Stampp's work, several studies have emphasized the importance of the slave community, slave religion, and slave culture in protecting individuals from the dehumanizing aspects of slavery. Among them is Eugene D. Genovese, *Roll Jordan Roll* (New York: Random House, 1974); John W. Blassingame, *The Slave Community: Plantation Life in the Ante-Bellum South* (New York: Oxford, 1972); Lawrence W. Levine, *Black Culture and Black Consciousness: Afro-American Folk Thought from Slavery to Freedom* (New York: Oxford, 1977); and Herbert G. Gutman, *The Black Family in Slavery and Freedom, 1750-1925* (New York: Random House, 1976). Significant interpretive overviews of American slavery have also been offered by Leslie Howard Owens, *This*

Species of Property: Slave Life and Culture in the Old South (New York: Oxford, 1976); C. Vann Woodward, *American Counterpoint: Slavery and Racism in the North-South Dialogue* (Boston: Little, Brown, 1971); Nathan Irvin Huggins, *Black Odyssey: The Afro-American Ordeal in Slavery* (New York: Random House, 1977); and Robert William Fogel and Stanley L. Engerman, *Time on the Cross: The Economics of American Negro Slavery* (Boston: Little, Brown, 1974).

Debates about the effects of slavery on race relations have provided a fiery battleground for historians. In a review of early colonial history Oscar and Mary Hardlin trace the origins of American racial slavery to economic needs in "Origins of the Southern Labor System," *William and Mary Quarterly* (April 1962). Carl N. Degler sees racial prejudice operating more independently in "Slavery and the Genesis of American Race prejudice," *Comparative Studies in Society and History* (October 1959). In *White Over Black: American Attitudes Toward the Negro, 1550-1812* (Chapel Hill: University of North Carolina, 1968) Winthrop D. Jordan suggests a reciprocal relationship but leans toward Degler's interpretation. George M. Fredrickson picks up the analysis of racial attitudes where Jordan leaves off and views the shift from environmental to biological perspectives in *The Black Image in the White Mind: The Debate on Afro-American Character and Destiny, 1817-1914* (New York: Harper and Row, 1971). William R. Stanton studies the emergence of prejudice based on "scientific" interpretations in *The Leopard's Spots: Scientific Attitudes Toward Race in America, 1815-1859* (Chicago: University of Chicago, 1960). Attitudes toward mulattoes are explored in James Hugo Johnson, *Race Relations in Virginia and Miscegenation in the South, 1770-1860* (Amherst, Mass.: University of Massachusetts, 1970); and Ira Berlin presents fascinating details about the status of mulattoes in *Slaves Without Masters: The Free Negro in the Antebellum South* (New York: Random House, 1974). Thomas F. Gosset offers a general review of racial ideology in *Race, The History of an Idea in America* (Dallas: Southern Methodist University, 1963). Also, the classic study by the Swedish scholar Gunnar Myrdal, *An American Dilemma: The Negro Problem and Modern Democracy*, 2 vols. (New York: Pantheon, 1975), remains useful for the way it places the problem of slavery in the larger context of race relations.

Two excellent general histories of the Afro-American experience trace the record from slavery to modern times. They are John Hope Franklin's *From Slavery to Freedom: A History of Negro Americans*, 3rd ed. (New York: Random House, 1967), and August Meir and Elliott Rudwick, *From Plantation to Ghetto*, rev. ed. (New York: Hill and Wang, 1970). Specific issues are addressed by an outstanding group of specialists in Afro-American history in Nathan I. Huggins, Martin Kilson, and Daniel M. Fox, *Key Issues In The*

Afro-American Experience, 2 vols. (New York: Harcourt, Brace, 1971). Important overviews of race relations since emancipation appear in John Hope Franklin, *Racial Equality in America* (Chicago: University of Chicago, 1976); C. Vann Woodward, *The Strange Career of Jim Crow* (New York: Oxford, 1959); August Meier and Elliott Rudwick, *Along the Color Line: Explorations in the Black Experience* (Urbana: University of Illinois, 1976); Oliver Cromwell Cox, *Race Relations: Elements and Dynamics* (Detroit: Wayne State University, 1976); E. Franklin Frazier, *The Negro in the United States* (Chicago: University of Chicago, 1966); George E. Simpson and J. Milton Yinger, *Racial and Cultural Minorities: An Analysis of Prejudice and Discrimination*, 4th ed. (New York: Harper and Row, 1972); Brewton Berry, *Race and Ethnic Relations* (Boston: Houghton Mifflin, 1958); Robert E. Park, *Race and Culture* (Glencoe, Ill.: Free Press, 1950); and Gary B. Nash and Richard Weiss, eds., *The Great Fear: Race in the Mind of America* (New York: Holt, Rinehart and Winston, 1970).

Discussions about the black man's difficult situation after emancipation have turned particularly to economic history in recent years. Interpretations of the failures of Reconstruction place heavy blame on the society's reluctance to distribute land to the freedmen. Among the important studies in this regard are Peter Camejo, *Racism, Revolution, Reaction, 1861-1877: The Rise and Fall of Radical Reconstruction* (New York: Monad, 1976); C. Peter Ripley, *Slaves and Freedmen in Civil War Louisiana* (Baton Rouge: Louisiana State University, 1976); Carl R. Osthaus, *Freedmen, Philanthropy, and Fraud: A History of the Freedman's Savings Bank* (Urbana: University of Illinois, 1976); Edward Magdol, *A Right to the Land: Essays on the Freedmen's Community* (Westport, Conn.: Greenwood, 1977); and Jay R. Mandle, *The Roots of Black Poverty* (Durham, N.C.: Duke University, 1978). Interpretations of the causes of black poverty also relate to assessments of the general economic condition of Southern agriculture after the Civil War. Robert Higgs argues that the Civil War was devastating to the South and that blacks suffered especially as victims of general economic difficulties rather than problems related specifically to their race. Higgs' views, which appear in *The Transformation of the American Economy, 1865-1914: An Essay in Interpretation* (New York: Wiley, 1971) and *Competition and Coercion: Blacks in the American Economy, 1865-1914* (Cambridge, England: Cambridge University, 1977), are challenged by Roger L. Random and Richard Sutch, *One Kind of Freedom: The Economic Consequences of Emancipation* (Cambridge, England: Cambridge University, 1977). Other dimensions of this important debate are intelligently reviewed by Pete Daniel in "The Metamorphosis of Slavery, 1865-1900" in *The Journal of American History* 66, no. 1 (June 1979), pp. 88-99.

Discrimination and segregation in the postwar South are discussed in C. Vann Woodward's now-classic study, *The Strange Career of Jim Crow* (New York: Oxford, 1959); and Howard N. Rabinowitz has published an excellent revisionist assessment of patterns of segregation in *Race Relations in the Urban South, 1865-1890* (New York: Oxford, 1978). The diversity of problems encountered by blacks in the difficult period from the Civil War to the Brown decision by the Supreme Court is reviewed in Allen Weinstein and Frank Otto Gatell, eds., *The Segregation Era, 1863-1954: A Modern Reader* (New York: Oxford, 1970).

The history of the civil rights movement in the United States has moved from journalism to scholarship in recent years. Anthony Lewis gives one of the best "on the scene" reports based on his coverage for the *New York Times* in *Portrait of a Decade* (New York: Bantam, 1964). More recently Earl Black showed the importance of the federal government's intervention in bringing change in *Southern Governors and Civil Rights: Racial Segregation as a Campaign Issue in the Second Reconstruction* (Cambridge, Mass.: Harvard University, 1976), and the political progress towards civil rights is discussed in Jack Bass and Walter De Vries, *The Transformation of Southern Politics: Social Change and Political Consequence Since 1945* (New York: Basic Books, 1976). Other writers place stronger emphasis on the continuing obstacles to change: Norman V. Bartley and Hugh Davis Graham, *Southern Politics and the Second Reconstruction* (Baltimore: Johns Hopkins, 1976); Steven F. Lawson, *Black Ballots: Voting Rights in the South, 1944-1969* (New York: Columbia University, 1976); and Neil R. McMillen, "Black Enfranchisement in Mississippi: Federal Enforcement and Black Protest in the 1960s," *Journal of Southern History* (August 1977), pp. 351-72.

The interpreters of economic change in the Second Reconstruction are also divided in their assessments of civil rights gains. Economist Thomas Sowell uses historical models to suggest hope for the future in *Race and Economics* (New York: Longman, 1975), and Ben Wattenberg finds encouraging statistical data in *The Real America: A Surprising Examination of the State of the Union* (New York: Paragon, 1976). Sar A. Levitan and other scholars are less sanguine in *Still a Dream: The Changing Status of Blacks Since 1960* (Cambridge, Mass.: Harvard University, 1975).

Gilberto Freyre's famous study, *The Masters and the Slaves: A Study in the Development of Brazilian Civilization* (New York: Random House, 1946), is a useful starting point for examining the debates over Brazilian slavery. Freyre is a sophisticated student of the subject, and his loosely worded comments about Brazil's "racial paradise" are not indicative of the complexity of his arguments. Freyre's description of the paternalism of Brazilian masters is challenged by C. R. Boxer's study of the gold-mining society, *The Golden*

Age of Brazil, 1690-1750: Growing Pains of a Colonial Society (Berkeley: University of California, 1962), and Stanley J. Stein's research on the coffee regions, *Vassouras: A Brazilian Coffee County, 1850-1900* (Cambridge, Mass.: Harvard University, 1957).

There are several excellent studies of specific issues in Brazilian slavery that are of interest for comparative study. Robert Conrad examines the status of freedmen in "Neither Slave Nor Free: The *Emancipados* of Brazil, 1818-1868," *Hispanic American Historical Review* (February 1973), pp. 50-70. Stuart B. Schwartz shows the conditions that could lead to rebellion in "Resistance and Accommodation in Eighteenth Century Brazil: The Slaves' View of Slavery," *Hispanic American Historical Review* (February 1977), pp. 68-81; and Thomas Flory studies the changing role of mulattoes in "Race and Social Control in Independent Brazil," *Journal of Latin American Studies* (November 1977).

The general history of the emancipation campaigns in Brazil are reviewed in Robert Brent Toplin, *The Abolition of Slavery in Brazil* (New York; Atheneum, 1972), and Robert Conrad, *The Destruction of Brazilian Slavery, 1850-1888* (Berkeley: University of California, 1972). Representative examples of the older and newer interpretations of abolition can be seen particularly in two articles: Percy Alvin Martin emphasizes the influence of reforms negotiated in parliament in "Slavery and Abolition in Brazil," *Hispanic American Historical Review* (February 1921), pp. 4-48; while Richard Graham underscores the importance of general economic changes, British influence, and violence on the plantations in "Causes of the Abolition of Negro Slavery in Brazil: An Interpretation," *Hispanic American Historical Review* (May 1966).

The consequences of abolition have been widely discussed in recent years. J. H. Galloway analyzes the connections between social, political, and economic attitudes in "The Last Years of Slavery on the Sugar Plantations of Northeast Brazil," *Hispanic American Historical Review* (November 1971), pp. 586-605; and Peter Eisenberg offers a different view of the same region in *The Sugar Industry in Pernambuco: Modernization Without Change, 1840-1910* (Berkeley: University of California, 1974). Warren Dean studies the impact of abolition in a coffee region of the south in *Rio Claro: A Brazilian Plantation System, 1820-1920* (Stanford: Stanford University, 1976). Some regional studies are especially valuable for the way they show the connections between abolition and postemancipation race relations. Among the important studies from scholars frequently identified as the "São Paulo School" are Emília Viotti da Costa, *Da senzala à colônia* (São Paulo: Difusão Européa, 1966); Octavio Ianni and Fernando Henrique Cardoso, *Côr e mobilidade em Florianópolis: Aspectos das relações êntre negros e brancos numa comunidade do Brasil meridional* (São Paulo, 1960); and Fernando Henrique Cardoso, *Capitalismo e escravidão: O negro na sociedade do Rio Grande do Sul* (São Paulo, 1962).

Gilberto Freyre's view of mild slavery and extensive social and sexual intermixing between black and white was explored in two important studies: Donald Pierson, *Negroes in Brazil: A Study of Race Contact at Bahia* (Chicago: University of Chicago, 1942), and Artur Ramos, *The Negro in Brazil* (Washington, D.C., 1939). More recently, interpretations have attacked Freyre on many fronts. Florestan Fernandes' ground-breaking research, which well summarizes the revisionist theme, has been translated into English: *The Negro in Brazilian Society* (New York: Columbia University, 1969). Rodger Bastide emphasizes the effects of job competition on racial thought in "Stereotypes, Norms, and Interracial Behavior in São Paulo Brazil," *American Sociological Review* 22, no. 6 (1957), pp. 689–94; and Bastide criticizes some of Melville J. Herskovits' ideas about African survivals in *African Civilizations in the New World* (London, 1971). Herskovits' famous study, *The Myth of the Negro Past* (Boston: Beacon, 1958), should be considered in this context. The complexity of Brazilian racial thought, especially among intellectuals, is brilliantly analyzed by Thomas E. Skidmore: *Black into White: Race and Nationality in Brazilian Thought* (New York: Oxford, 1974); and Charles Wagley shows the interrelationships of class and color factors in the formation of prejudice in *Amazon Town: A Study of Man in the Tropics*, rev. ed. (New York: Random House, 1976), and *An Introduction to Brazil*, rev. ed. (New York, Columbia University, 1971). Some of the criticisms of Freyre's work have been particularly sharp in recent years. Thales de Azevedo reviews the case for revisionism in *Democracia racial: ideologia e realidade* (Petropolis, 1975), and Abdias do Nascimento presents hard-hitting attacks on Brazil's traditions of subtle discrimination in *O negro revoltado* (Rio de Janeiro: Edições GDR, 1968) and *O genocídio do negro brasileiro* (Rio de Janeiro, 1977).

Index

About the Author

ROBERT BRENT TOPLIN is Associate Professor of History at the University of North Carolina at Wilmington. His earlier books include *The Abolition of Slavery in Brazil* (1972) and two published by Greenwood Press: *Slavery and Race Relations in Latin America* (1974) and *Unchallenged Violence: An American Ordeal* (1975).